ELECTION BY LOT
AT ATHENS

ELECTION BY LOT
AT ATHENS

BY THE LATE

JAMES WYCLIFFE HEADLAM, M.A.
(J. W. HEADLAM-MORLEY)

FELLOW OF KING'S COLLEGE, CAMBRIDGE

Second edition revised by

D. C. MACGREGOR

FELLOW OF BALLIOL COLLEGE, OXFORD

PRINCE CONSORT DISSERTATION, 1890

CAMBRIDGE

AT THE UNIVERSITY PRESS

1933

CAMBRIDGE
UNIVERSITY PRESS

University Printing House, Cambridge CB2 8BS, United Kingdom

Cambridge University Press is part of the University of Cambridge.

It furthers the University's mission by disseminating knowledge in the pursuit of
education, learning and research at the highest international levels of excellence.

www.cambridge.org
Information on this title: www.cambridge.org/9781107658653

First edition 1891
Second edition 1933
First published 1933
First paperback edition 2014

A catalogue record for this publication is available from the British Library

ISBN 978-1-107-65865-3 Paperback

EXTRACT FROM THE REGULATIONS FOR THE PRINCE CONSORT PRIZE.

"There shall be established in the University a prize, called the 'Prince Consort Prize,' to be awarded for dissertations involving original historical research."

"The prize shall be open to members of the University who, at the time when their dissertations are sent in, have been admitted to a degree, and are of not more than four years' standing from admission to their first degree."

"Those dissertations which the adjudicators declare to be deserving of publication shall be published by the University, singly or in combination, in an uniform series, at the expense of the fund, under such conditions as the Syndics of the University Press shall from time to time determine."

PATRI CARISSIMO

PREFACE.

THE subject treated of in this Essay cannot be entirely passed over in any book dealing with Greek Political Antiquities or History. Whether it be owing to the obscurity of the matter, or to some other cause, the explanations given in the standard works are neither sufficient nor convincing. I have therefore attempted by devoting a more special study to the subject than can be done in larger books, to see how far the information we have is sufficient to enable us to understand exactly what election by lot was, how it was used, and what were its political effects.

I am not aware of the existence of any article specially devoted to the subject. So far as attention has been paid to it, it has been confined to one, and, as it seems to me, the least important part of the matter. The date and occasion of the introduction of the lot for elections to the archonship is one of those questions which is at least referred to in all books dealing with Athenian history. It appears as though the exaggerated importance attached to what is to a great extent an antiquarian point, has distracted the attention of most writers from what is at least of equal interest, the political effects of the very much extended use of the lot in later times.

This is the more to be regretted because it seems as though the discussion of the first point could not lead to any satisfactory conclusion. Our knowledge of the end of the 6th and the beginning of the 5th century is so fragmentary, that, unless some new source of information is discovered, we can do nothing but make clever guesses. On the other hand, an understanding of the use of the lot from the middle of the 5th century onwards is essential, if we are to form any true conception of the nature of the Athenian Democracy; and the great amount of contemporary material which we possess, both in books and inscriptions, ought to enable us at least to get somewhere near the truth.

This limitation of view is found where we should least expect it,—even in Grote, Curtius, and Busolt. These and other historians almost completely neglect to explain the application of the lot to the council and other offices; and yet some explanation is surely wanted. The few monographs which touch the matter at all are almost exclusively occupied with the antiquarian question. The longest of these is an article by *Lugebil*, who was formerly professor at Petersburg University. The article was originally written in Russian, but has since appeared in German[1]. The author has lately died, and so without entering on any detailed criticism it will be sufficient to say that little is to be gained by reading it. The learning and research which it

---

[1] In the Jahrbuch f. kl. Philologie, Suppl. Band, v. 1871.

contains are deprived of nearly all their value by the disproportionate length given to inconclusive discussions of unimportant points.

Fustel de Coulanges[1] is another writer who has paid special attention to one part of the subject. As is so often the case he has with admirable clearness put forward an explanation which if it does not contain, as he seems to think, the whole truth, is certainly an important part of the truth.

To *Müller-Strübing*[2] belongs the merit of attempting a thorough discussion of the political question. It is unfortunate that his merit does not go farther. As I shall attempt to show later, both his method and conclusions are radically wrong. His cleverness and ability belong rather to a political pamphleteer than to a scholar. His work is seriously marred by a deplorable absence of sound judgment or power of self-criticism. This is made more conspicuous by the very low estimate he makes of the work of men in every way his superior.

In attempting to find a satisfactory explanation of the lot, I have necessarily been compelled to form and state an opinion not only on various minor points connected with it, but also on the political working of the constitution as a whole. In doing so I have constantly referred to the books of *Gilbert*[3]

[1] In La Cité antique, and an article in the Nouvelle Revue Historique de la Droit 1882. The article does not add much of importance to the short statement made in the first-named work.

[2] In Aristophanes und die historische Kritik.

[3] Beiträge zur inneren Geschichte Athens, and Griechische Staatsalterthümer

H. *b*

and *Beloch*[1]. The first volume of Gilbert's "Staatsalterthümer" I have found especially valuable.
They have both been extremely useful to me in the
discussion of many details; even when I have
differed from them I have still learned from them
what is often of most importance, a clear perception
of the existence of a difficulty. It is the more
necessary for me to say this because I seldom refer
to them except when I differ from them: and in fact
the greater part of this essay would not have been
written, had I not found in their books theories on
the Athenian constitution maintained, which appeared very misleading.

It is scarcely necessary to acknowledge the debt
which in common with all classical students I owe
to Boeckh, Hermann, and Schömann. The more
one studies them the more apparent are not only
the accuracy and learning, but also the wisdom and
insight of these great scholars. They have that large
grasp and clear perception of the mode of Greek life
which gives to their work a permanent value, even
if their conclusions on numerous minor points have
been superseded, or corrected. Hence they are (as
it seems to me) even when they have to be corrected,
far safer guides than more modern authors, who
often make the mistake of exaggerating the importance of some new discovery or hypothesis, and in

---

[1] Die Attische Politik seit Perikles.

I ought to add Mr Whibley's book on "Political Parties at
Athens" published in this series, which drew my attention to
many interesting points. To it too I owe my first acquaintance
with much of the modern literature on the subject.

doing so have missed or ignored some simple and
natural explanation which is to be found in Hermann
or Schömann. This characteristic of the modern
writers has at times obliged me to prove at some
length points which to those unacquainted with
their works would appear self-evident. The cause
of this decline (for this it must be called) appears to
be that while the older authors were willing to
learn from the Greeks, and were content to follow
Thucydides, Plato, and Aristotle, repeating and explaining their judgments, the modern writers aim
at criticising and correcting them. And yet, without
maintaining that those writers were infallible, it is
still true that the more we study Greek life the
more evident it is that not only in personal knowledge of the society in which they lived, but also in
the power of analysing its constitution and characteristics, they are unsurpassed. Only those who have
had to read the modern literature on the subject know
how wearisome is the attempt of each new writer
to display his own acumen by finding fault with
them. One of the most common causes of much
of their criticism is a mistaken ingenuity in the
application of modern political experience to the
explanation of Greek politics. This method, which
was used with such admirable results by Grote, has
been a false guide to many who having neither his
practical experience, nor his quick intuition in dealing with political matters, write as though the
phenomena of the Athenian ecclesia can at once be
explained by a second-hand acquaintance with the
proceedings of some German representative assembly.

As books of reference, besidès Gilbert's Staatsalterthümer I have made special use of the article
by *Busolt* on Griechische Alterthümer in Vol. IV. of
Iwan Müller's Handbuch der Klassischen Alterthums-
wissenschaft, and the volumes of his history. Both
are especially useful for their full bibliography. My
chief authorities are of course the ordinary classical
texts, especially the contemporary writers, such as
Aristophanes and the Orators. Important as is the
information preserved by second-hand authorities
such as Plutarch and the Lexicographers, these later
writers had only a very limited knowledge of the
Athenian constitution, and they had few opportunities for becoming acquainted with the working of
free institutions.

The information gained from inscriptions on the
other hand is most valuable. They supplement
the literary tradition by exposing to us aspects of
political life which are not treated of in the books
at all. It is to be hoped that, using them, someone
will complete the work begun by Boeckh, and rewrite
the account of the Athenian constitution and administration, thus doing for it what Mommsen has
done for Rome. In dealing with them, besides the
Corpus I have constantly used Boeckh's Staatshaushaltung[1], Hicks' Manual of Greek Historical Inscriptions, and Dittenberger's Sylloge. The delay in the
appearance of the index to the second volume of the
Corpus has caused much inconvenience.

Other books and articles which I have used

---

[1] I have used the new edition admirably edited by Fränkel.
I may also mention *Pape's* Lexicon der Griechischen Eigennamen.

occasionally will be found referred to in the footnotes.

_____

So far I had written before it became known
that the πολιτεία τῶν Ἀθηναίων of Aristotle had
been discovered. As however the whole of the essay
and introduction had been in type for some weeks,
and much of it was nearly ready for the press before
the new work was published, I have been obliged to
leave both unchanged. They appear therefore exactly
as they were written, and I have since then made no
alterations of any kind in the text or notes, except
linguistic corrections. I have added in an appendix
a few notes in which I have pointed out the places in
which the statement of the text will require alteration, and also those in which the view I have taken
of doubtful matters is corroborated. In most cases
references to the appendix will be found inserted in
square brackets: as I had to insert many of them
before the appendix was written they must not be
taken as in any way a complete guide to it. I have
attempted in this way so far as possible to incorporate
the new information in this work: and the task has
been less difficult than I had anticipated, because the
πολιτεία, so far as it touches on the matters with which
I am dealing, seems to confirm the view I have taken
of the working of the Athenian constitution. The
argument of the main body of the essay remains
therefore valid. Had the πολιτεία appeared a year
earlier, I should hardly have felt it necessary to give
such a lengthy discussion on a point which is now I
hope conclusively established by it. I should es-

pecially like to call attention to the passage quoted
in the appendix, in which for the first time we get a
definite statement of the principle for which I have
argued, that the lot was used to secure rotation in
office.

The πολιτεία consists of two portions; one a
history of the constitution of Athens down to the
year 403, the other an account of the constitution
in the form known personally to the writer, written
between the years 327 and 322[1].

The first of these two divisions is of particular
interest because it supplies just the information
which was wanting as to the early history of the lot.
This subject I have discussed in the appendix to
Ch. II.; the new information will be found in the
notes at the end; it will be seen that we now
have an authoritative statement on a matter with
regard to which (as I said above, p. x) the absence
of evidence seemed to have brought all further
discussion to a stand-still. It is of course some
satisfaction to me that on the main point the view
I had supported is confirmed.

Next to this the most important part in the first
section is the full account given of the constitutional
policy of the party of Theramenes. This only indirectly bears on my subject.

It is difficult at once to decide exactly how much

[1] The latter date is fixed because the book must have been
written before the change in the constitution made after the
Lamian war.

Mr Cecil Torr in the *Athenæum* for Feb. 7, attempts to fix the
latest date still more closely, because in ch. 46 there is no
mention of πεντηρεῖς, which were first used in 325.

that is new we learn from the second statistical section. The value of it is to some extent diminished because we have to be very careful not to argue directly from the statements contained in it, to the state of things which prevailed in the earlier period of the democracy. It is indeed a serious defect of the book that it gives no account of the administration, and little of the constitution, during the times of Pericles and the Peloponnesian war. This is the more serious for my purpose because I have attributed great importance to the changes supposed to have been made about the year 350, by the introduction of new elective finance offices. Much that is contained in this section was familiar to us before, because it is from it that the Lexicographers have borrowed—as appears often inaccurately. The defect in the work to which I have already referred, explains also how it is that these later writers tell so little of the constitution of the 5th century. They depended on Aristotle and the orators: and we learn little more about the 5th century from the former than we do from the latter.

One result of the discovery of this work will be, I imagine, to add considerably to Plutarch's reputation. Where they go over the same ground, it will I think be found that Plutarch has used his Aristotle very intelligently, so much so that his life of Solon may be used for determining the text; and has also at times used the same authorities as Aristotle in such a way that he supplements and perhaps even corrects him—but on this it is impossible yet to give a decided opinion.

In conclusion I must express my thanks to Mr
A. A. Tilley, Fellow of King's College and University
Lecturer in Roman History, who has kindly read the
proofs of a considerable portion of the Essay; to
Professor Pelham, one of the adjudicators for the
Prince Consort Prize, for some useful criticisms on
the earlier portions; and especially to my cousin Mr
C. E. S. Headlam, Fellow of Trinity Hall, who has
given me the most generous help in passing the
essay through the Press. But for his constant advice
and assistance it would be disfigured by defects even
more serious than those which remain.

KING'S COLLEGE, CAMBRIDGE,
    February 26, 1891.

PREFACE TO THE SECOND EDITION.

Election by Lot at Athens was awarded the Prince Consort Prize in 1890, and very quickly won for itself an international reputation such as seldom waits upon Prize Essays. Abroad, Thumser[1]—who gave a long and masterly summary of its contents—reviewed it in terms of the very liveliest admiration and respect, and professed himself in entire agreement with the essentials of its teaching. In England, Dr Macan[2] wrote of it: "No writer has better understood and expressed the spirit ($\mathring{\eta}\theta os$) of the Athenian democracy and its constitution." It need hardly be said that these are

---

[1] *Berl. Phil. Wochenschr.* 1891, 1490 ff. Thumser frequently cites it in his edition of Hermann (1892). P. Meyer (*Neue Phil. Rundschau*, 1892, p. 370 ff.) writes in the same sense. (His remarks on the literary presentation of the book are perhaps worth quoting: "Das Ganze ist mit sehr grosser Klarheit und Folgerichtigkeit recht anschaulich durchgeführt nicht im Geschmack der deutschen Systematiker, sondern mehr von dem Streben beherrscht, ein einigermassen abgerundetes Kunstwerk zu liefern. Das einzige, was zu erinnern wäre, ist einer nach deutschen Begriffe etwas zu grosse Breite." [One is reminded of Boeckh's outburst: Ich hasse die Breitheit womit besonders die ausländischen Gelehrten sich über die Inschriften ergiessen.] "Man muss diese indes dem Streben seinen Hauptgedanken zu möglichst klarer Anschauung zu bringen einigermassen zu gut halten.") The other reviews recorded in Bursian for 1892 and 1893 are equally laudatory. In 1894 Hans Keller published his careful and sincere *Studien zum Attischen Staatsrecht*, in which he acknowledges his debt to Headlam in terms of the utmost deference.

[2] *Classical Review*, 1892.

not ignorant or capricious criticisms, but deliberate judgements of men who knew what they were speaking of. In fact Headlam-Morley—Headlam, as he then was —seemed to have taken his place at once in the small and good company of notable Hellenists. But he did not keep it long. His own defection to other fields of study no doubt had something to do with it; but in fact the time was inopportune. The attention of scholars was excited and absorbed by the manifold problems created or revived by the publication in 1891 of the Ἀθηναίων Πολιτεία. It was a decade of many large and important books—and one great book—concerned for the most part with the new discovery; and an essay which dealt with it only in a short and hurried appendix, and which in any case was more concerned with the understanding of the general principles of government in Athens than with the solution of new problems of detail, was only too easily set aside as an irrelevance. Moreover, there were then too many scholars—there are happily fewer now—whose attitude to the study of political institutions was wholly irreconcilable with Headlam's. This may be conveniently illustrated by comparing his remark on pp. 80–81, "It is absurd to discuss a political institution apart from its surroundings as if it were an abstract expression," with Heisterbergk's retort[1] (p. viii), "dass es ebensowenig zulässig sei, in einer Institution, welche sich unter verschiedenen Verfassungsformen dauernd erhalten hat, nur den

---

[1] *Die Bestellung der Beamten durch das Los* (1896). This ingenious and obtuse book is not a heartening advertisement of the method which it advocates.

Spiegel ihrer jeweiligen Umgebung sehen zu wollen, als ob sie eines eigenen Inhalts ermangelt hätte." To those who have an appetite for this kind of political study there was little nourishment in Headlam. And finally, although no book is more accurately adjusted to the real needs of Greek history teaching in schools and universities, *Election by Lot at Athens* was not of the kind which is believed to be educational.

Whether these considerations explain it or not, the second edition to which Dr Macan looked forward was never called for; the book was allowed to slip away from the good company which had welcomed it, and to drop into the underworld of footnotes and bibliographies. Even from that world it has almost entirely disappeared[1]; and Professor Zimmern had sufficiently forgotten it to write that it was "still worth *consulting* for its practical insight into the *detailed* working of the Athenian government[2]." Now a book may drop out of memory and no one be seriously the worse, provided that its wisdom does not die with it. But that has happened here. However much he may disagree with him, any careful and

[1] It is mentioned—and neglected—in Greenidge's *Handbook of Greek Constitutional History*; in Glotz's *Sortitio* (*Dict. des Antiquités*) it is not even mentioned. It has recently been rescued by Ehrenberg, who made good use of it in his most excellent and judicious article *Losung* (*R.E.* vol. xiii).

[2] *The Greek Commonwealth*, p. 164 note. (The italics are not his.) It would be difficult to misrepresent the book with more deadly precision. It is a book without which no historian's library is complete; but it must not be placed among the works of reference. "Practical insight," however, is sound enough.

candid reader must admit that Headlam has been
able to give an account of the lot and an interpretation of Athenian government which are self-consistent
and consonant both with the known antiquarian facts
and with human nature in politics; and that he
thereby created a new obligation upon historians to
treat the lot not as an insignificant oddity, but as an
institution which, with its modifications and rare
exceptions, must—however interpreted—be kept in
the forefront of attention in any study of Athenian
democracy; as something which was in actual fact so
natural and necessary to the Athenians that over a
period of many generations it survived success and
catastrophe and revolution, and even survived the
active criticism of the influential thinkers and statesmen who disapproved it. To this extent at least
Election by Lot at Athens should have been a
prolegomenon to every future political or social history
of Athens. Nevertheless, the books in common use
to-day[1] are still content to say that the lot was used;
but that sensible men like Socrates saw it to be an
absurdity, and that even the Athenian people safeguarded itself in practice against its caprices; and
that, not to put too fine a point upon it, it was not quite
as bad as it sounds—and having said so much or so
little, they proceed to study the course of Athenian
history as though the lot had never existed. The

---

[1] The chapter on Athens in Bryce's *Modern Democracies* is a
welcome exception in this regard, and—short as it is—gives a
much less misleading picture of Athenian government than the
professional histories. But even it scarcely comes to grips with
the question.

decision of the Syndics of the Press to put *Election by Lot at Athens* again into circulation may do a service to learning far greater than the mere resuscitation of a forgotten book.

The present edition is a photolithographic reproduction of the original with only such corrections of misprints, false references and the like, as the nature of the process allowed. All the references to the ancient authorities have been checked, and nearly all those to modern works—though of these a few *loca senta situ* have been left undisturbed. Although some of the editions to which Headlam referred are no longer in use, it has not always seemed necessary to substitute references to later editions; but the passage from the *Corpus Inscriptionum Atticarum* to more accessible collections is so dismally wasteful of time that a *comparatio numerorum* has been drawn up for the reader's comfort[1]. A few short notes have been added (Appendix II); but narrowness of space made it impossible to attempt to do more: indeed, it was neither necessary nor desirable. Headlam's insight and grasp of principle were such that his theory has for the most part been confirmed when confronted with new evidence of detail; and his book is in no sense that matters out of date[2]—

[1] Mr M. N. Tod, *pro sua comitate*, allowed me access before publication to his *Greek Historical Inscriptions*. For this and for other kindness I am deeply grateful to him.

[2] One might fairly say that Headlam's was an ideal construction to which the Athens of fact approximated *as nearly as it could*. He knew this himself, and allowed for it throughout. Later work, of which much the most important is that of Sundwall (*Epigraphische Beiträge*), has shown that in certain respects the approximation

with the one exception of the note to Chapter II. This has been antiquated by the ᾿Αθηναίων Πολιτεία, and by the subsequent analysis of many scholars. But Headlam himself regarded these problems of the earlier history as of subordinate interest (p. ix); and anyone who has no new thesis to defend, and so can contemplate, *sine ira et studio*, the rival theories of others, will agree that nothing was to be gained by burdening this book with excrescent accounts of them[1]. These problems in fact involve too many unknowns; and in spite of the more than Diophantine ingenuity expended on them they remain insoluble[2].

D. C. M.

BALLIOL COLLEGE.
January 9, 1933.

was not so close as Headlam had supposed; and doubtless in course of time other discoveries will be made which will reveal other small discrepancies in detail between theory and observational fact. But hitherto, at least, nothing has come to light which invalidates or antiquates the general theory.

[1] For sustained ingenuity Ledl's analysis in *Studien zur älteren athenischen Verfassungsgeschichte*, p. 339 ff., stands perhaps highest of all; but it cannot be said to settle the matter. Ehrenberg's *Lösung* (*op. cit.*) gives an admirable summary of recent attempts, and suggests tentatively what seems to him the most probable solution.

[2] A dagger † indicates those passages to which I have added a note.

CONTENTS.

CHAPTER I.

CHAPTER VI.

CHAPTER VII.

APPENDIX.

CHAPTER I.

Introduction.

THERE is no institution of ancient history which is so difficult of comprehension as that of electing officials by the lot. We have ourselves no experience of the working of such a system; any proposal to introduce it now would appear so ludicrous that it requires some effort for us to believe that it ever did prevail in a civilised community. There can be few people who, when they first hear that it existed at Athens and in other Greek states, do not receive the information with incredulity. The first impulse is to doubt the fact and to suppose there is some misunderstanding. And there have been scholars who have attempted to show that election by lot did not exist; that what is commonly known as such was really secret voting by ballot. The attempt fails; for the evidence of the authorities is overwhelming[1].

Other historians recognising the fact of election by lot have treated it as a matter of no great importance; without explicitly saying so, they seem to hold that its effects were not great because the chief

---

[1] See an article in the Philological Museum, vol. ii., apparently by Sir G. C. Lewis, referring to an attempt of this kind.

offices in the state were filled in some other way:
they point out truly enough that when an office such
as the Archonship which in earlier times was filled
by popular election came to be filled by lot, it ceased
to be of any political importance; and hence they
conclude that if numerous minor administrative posts
were so filled, the custom is curious and rather
foolish, it is characteristic of the democratic jealousy,
but did not seriously affect the government of the
state. That was in the hands of men elected by the
Assembly. This view is natural and recommends
itself to our common sense : it contains this amount
of truth that of all the officials elected by lot there
is no single one who stands out above the others as
entrusted with especially weighty duties. But it
ignores, what is equally true, that, though no individual office is of particular prominence, the work
done by all the officials elected by lot was together
of the greatest extent. It is scarcely too much to
say that the whole administration of the state was
in the hands of men appointed by lot : the serious
work of the law courts, of the execution of the laws,
of police, of public finance, in short of every department (with the exception of actual commands in the
army) was done by officials so chosen. And, what is
still more surprising, the council before which all
public business passed ; the council which was the
only permanent governing body in the state, which
had superintendence of financial matters, through
which negotiations with foreign powers were conducted, this too was chosen by the lot. The whole
business of the city, with the exception of that small

portion which could be directly decided on by the Assembly, was in the hands of men selected by " chance."

The more closely we analyse the working of the Athenian state, the more universal appears the operation of the lot, and the greater appears the anomaly. This has led other scholars to suggest as a solution of the difficulty that election by lot was not really what we should suppose ; names were indeed put into an urn and drawn out by the Archon; but this was only a convenient veil ; the result was not really left to chance : many names might be put in, but it was well known beforehand which name would come out ; there were recognised conventions by which the whole thing was worked. A returning officer who did not use his discretion would have failed in his duty. Unfortunately this view also, attractive though it is, fails, as did that mentioned above, from the complete absence of evidence. I believe I am right in saying that there is not a single particle of evidence in any classical writer which justifies us in supposing that the result of the lot was not really the verdict of chance ; still less that the whole community was aware of the existence of any such understanding[1].

Another method of explaining away the difficulty is to suppose that although the lot did really decide between the different candidates for any post, yet there was not really much left to chance, because the number of candidates was in one way or another strictly limited ; either we may suppose that each

[1] Cf. infra, p. 54 n. 1 and 2.

candidate must be nominated, or that public opinion was strong enough to prevent unsuitable persons becoming candidates.

I shall content myself with mentioning this view here; I shall refer to it again later, when I believe I shall be able to show that there was (at least in the times after Pericles) no important restriction of this kind to the free action of the lot; had such existed it would have been an effectual check on the objects for which the lot was introduced.

I propose therefore to enquire what were the reasons for which the Athenians adopted a custom so strange, and also to examine what were the effects of it on the political system of which it formed a part. It is scarcely necessary to point out that, without an explanation of this matter, we cannot hope thoroughly to understand or appreciate the nature of the Athenian Democracy; and I hope the enquiry, even if it is of no other use, will help to draw attention to some peculiarities of the administrative system and will thereby throw light on certain tendencies which seem to be essential to democratic government.

The connection of the lot with religious beliefs. But before I discuss the first question, what political advantages were supposed to come from the use of the lot, it is necessary to consider a suggestion which, if true, would greatly alter the character of the enquiry. It is often maintained that the essence of the lot was religious. If this were true then we should have to consider it as we do omens and oracles; it would be another case of an old superstition interfering with the political life of the

people; its preservation would be another instance
of that deep-rooted conservatism in all that concerned their worship which often reminds us that
the Athenians were not all philosophers or sceptics.

It is well established that in early stages of
society the lot is regarded as one among many ways
through which the Gods give counsel and advice to
men. This was the case both in Greece and Italy.
The Greek lived in constant intercourse with his
Gods; for every work which he began and every
decision which he made he looked to them for
advice and guidance. He required some hint as to
the result of his labours or some sanction for his
enterprise. And the drawing or casting of lots was
always one way in which this communication took
place. This is abundantly proved from the times of
Homer down to the latest days of the Roman
Empire: and, as might reasonably have been expected, the lot was chiefly used when the matter
on which the Gods were consulted was the choice
either of some man from a limited number to receive
certain honours or perform certain duties, or the
division among a few men of an equal number of
duties.

The best illustration of this is the fact that *Priests*
throughout Greece it was the regular custom to use *appointed by lot.*
the lot for the appointment of priests and others
who ministered in the temples[1]. There is no doubt
that this was done because it was held fitting that
the God himself should choose those who were to

[1] Cf. Jules Martha, Les Sacerdoces Athéniens in the Bibl. des
Écoles Francaises, xxvi. 1882. pp. 30—35.

serve him. If he had not declared his pleasure by an omen or a dream, an opinion could always be secured by the use of the lot. This custom prevailed till the latest times, and though it had probably become a mere ritual observance, it is at least a sign that the appointment of a priest had not the highest validity unless it had received the express sanction of the God.

It is easy then to assume that the lot which was so essential a part of the religious ceremonial retained its religious significance when used for political purposes; and even to draw the conclusion that the religious belief was really the chief reason why it was so extensively used. There is nothing in what we know of Athenian habits of thought to make this improbable; whatever may have been the opinions of a few educated men, there is no doubt that the great mass of the people firmly believed in the continual intervention of the Gods in the affairs of men. They were not ashamed, nor were they frightened, to allow affairs of the greatest moment to be influenced by dreams, omens, portents and oracles. They were guided by these in private and public life alike[1]. We should therefore be quite prepared to find that the use of the lot in state affairs

[1] Perhaps the most remarkable illustration of this is contained in one of the speeches of Hypereides. We there find the Assembly solemnly ordering three men to go and sleep in a temple in order that one of them might learn in a dream the opinion of Amphiaraus on a disputed point of property (Or. iii pro Euxenippo, xxvii—viii.† It is only necessary to refer to the Anabasis and Hellenica of Xenophon for instances of the readiness with which men would incur the greatest dangers rather than neglect an omen.

was, at least by the great mass of the people, upheld because they wished thereby to get the sanction of the Gods for the appointment of their officials.

This view becomes still more plausible when we remember that the most conspicuous of the officials so appointed were the nine Archons; men who had special religious duties and still represented in their office the old union of priest and magistrate. And the state worship at Athens was so closely connected with the public functions that even though the newer offices did not have the same religious importance as the Archonship, it is easy to suppose that the pious Athenians liked to have the same divine sanction extended also to those who filled them[1].

This however will not really explain our difficulty. The explanation has been put forward[2] by those who have confined their attention to the Archonship and have not sufficiently appreciated the reality and extent of the use of the lot. It may be true that there was a religious sentiment which made the

[1] Cf. Lugebil, l. c. p. 666 etc.

[2] Fustel de Coulanges, Nouvelle Revue Historique de Droit, ii. 1878, p. 617—643 ; and La Cité antique, p. 213. "Le caractère sacerdotal qui s'attachait au magistrat se montre surtout dans la manière dont il était élu. Aux yeux des anciens, il ne semblait pas que les suffrages des hommes fussent suffisants pour établir le chef de la cité. Les hommes paraissent avoir cherché, pour suppléer à la naissance, un mode d'élection que les dieux n'eussent pas à désavouer. Les Athéniens, comme beaucoup de peuples grecs, n'en virent pas de meilleur que le tirage de sort. Pour eux le sort n'était pas le hasard ; le sort était la révélation de la volonté divine." He gives no illustrations of this except two passages from the Laws of Plato. Cf. p. 8 n. 1.

common people cling to the lot, and it could have
happened that far-sighted statesmen used this to help
in carrying out their policy, but it will not explain
why statesmen who certainly were not influenced by
religious conservatism wished to extend the use of it,
nor how it was that the state which used it could
possibly exist and prosper. What evidence there is
for the view is, I believe, entirely confined to passages which speak of the Archonship, and, as I shall
show, the use of the lot for this was only a small and
scarcely the most important part of its application.

Use of the
lot at
Athens
cannot be
explained
by refer-
ence to
religious
beliefs.
The fact is that at Athens where the use of
the lot was most common the evidence for its religious signification is smallest. This can be seen
by the small number of references put forward by
those who maintain this view. I believe the only
passages which expressly refer to the lot as giving
religious sanction to an appointment are two which
occur in the Laws of Plato[1]; and it will be sufficient
to point out that the constitution of the ideal state
which the philosopher is describing is essentially
different from that of Athens, and that he is in
the second of the two passages expressly showing
how different is his ideal from the " equality " of a
democracy. He is gravely reminding his readers of
what the lot ought to be. Everyone will agree that
the lot could be regarded as a religious institution,
and that it had been such in old times, but nevertheless after the beginning of the fifth century it
does not appear to have been so regarded at Athens.

This is shown even by the poets. In the Tra-

[1] Plato, Leges iii. 690ᶜ; vi. 757ᵈ.†

gedians mention is often made of the lot; and occasionally in such words that we are reminded it had a religious origin. But this is only the case when it is mentioned in direct connection with the services of some temple[1]. In no other cases is it spoken of as religious; and never do we find attaching to its use the awe and mystery which belongs to other more impressive means of divine utterance. Even in Æschylus it has none of the associations which belong to oracles and dreams. Still more is this true of Euripides. We find in the Heracleidae one striking instance of this "secularisation" of the lot. Macaria says she is willing to be made a sacrifice to Demeter, who has demanded the offering of a maiden. Iolaus demurs. He represents that it would be juster if she and her sisters drew lots, and selected the victim in this way. But Macaria will not hear of this; such a death would not please her.

οὐκ ἂν θάνοιμι τῇ τύχῃ λαχοῦσ' ἐγώ·
χάρις γὰρ οὐ πρόσεστι[2].

It would be wanting in the graciousness which belongs to a voluntary sacrifice. And Euripides does not think it necessary to put into the mouth of either of his characters the suggestion that to submit to the will of the goddess expressed in this way would be even more gracious than self-willed to force oneself upon her[3].

This and similar passages do not go far: but

[1] Eur. Ion, 416. Æsch. Eum. 32.
[2] Eur. Heracleidae 547.
[3] Mr Frazer in the Golden Bough gives an account of an old

they are some evidence that the religious feeling connected with the lot was, even in a matter directly connected with the gods, extremely weak, and point to the fact, not that the political use of the lot was a religious ceremony, but that the constant use of it for secular purposes had almost completely destroyed the old religious associations.

So when Socrates freely expressed contempt for the lot, this was made the ground for a charge of political discontent, but it is never referred to as connected with the accusations of atheism. And the speeches of the orators afford stronger testimony to the same phenomenon. These clever men who are so ready to use every fallacy likely to be effective and appeal to every prejudice or commonplace likely to give them the appearance of right, never once, in the speeches which are preserved, allude to the lot as sacred; and this though the audience they were addressing was in nearly every case selected by the lot. The absence of such a reference is sometimes startling. There is a passage in Deinarchus where he makes a passionate appeal to the dicasts to condemn Philocles. "The people," he says, "have deprived this man of his office; they did not think it right or safe that he should longer have the care of their children, and

custom which used to prevail in many parts of Scotland; pieces of dough, one of which is blackened, are put into a hat; the inhabitants one after another take each one of the pieces blindfolded out of the hat. The one who draws the black piece is a victim. He is not now burnt, but part of the company make a show of putting him into the fire. Vol. ii. p. 255—6.

will you, you who are guardians of the democracy
and the laws, you whom chance and the lot have
appointed to give justice for the people, will you
spare him[1]?" If he could have done so without
being ridiculous would not Deinarchus have said
θεός not τύχη? It is scarcely too much to say that
not only did neither he nor his audience believe in
the religious connections of the lot, but that they
did not even pretend to do so.

For this is not a single case. We have for †
instance a speech by Lysias written in defence of a
man who had been appointed βουλευτής, but had
been accused on his δοκιμασία[2]. He had been appointed by the lot: his opponents wished to unseat
him on political grounds. Lysias never uses the
obvious topic, he never warns his hearers that the
man whom the lot has selected has acquired a
peculiar right, and that to undo his appointment
without due cause is a form of sacrilege.

The conclusion I draw from these facts is that *Conclu-
the lot was religious in its origin, and that it was to *sion.*
the latest times throughout Greece used in the
ritual of the temples with a clear acknowledgment
that its decision gave a divine sanction; but that at
Athens owing to its constant use for political purposes it was secularised till almost all recollection
of its religious origin had disappeared; that the
statesmen who developed the system in which it
was used were not themselves guided by religious
beliefs, and that, even if they were to some extent
helped by a certain superstitious feeling among the

---

[1] Deinarchus, in Philoclen 15—16.   [2] Lysias, pro Mantitheo.

poorer people, this was in no way the decisive cause of the success of their policy. Soon amidst all the busy political and legal life at Athens what there was of religious feeling about it died out. It was at Rome where it was seldom used, not at Athens where it influenced the life of every citizen, that men talked of the "religio sortis[1]."

We can then return to our original question: What was the object and effect of the extended use of the lot as it prevailed during the fifth and fourth centuries? and I shall attempt to show how the Athenian statesmen used this relic of a dying super-stition as the means of carrying out with remarkable vigour their political ideals.

The lot demo-cratic. For whatever may be our difficulties the Greeks themselves seem to have had no doubt why the lot was used at Athens, nor what its effect was. On this they are explicit. Election by lot was a demo-cratic institution; more, it was necessary to a demo-cracy. In this they are almost unanimous; friends and enemies of democracy all agree on this point that in a perfectly democratic state magistrates will

---

[1] It is only necessary to read Fustel de Coulanges' account of the democracy (La Cité antique, iv. ch. 11) to see how impossible his theory is. It leads him to a direct misstatement of fact when he says "Les magistrats prêtres étaient choisis par le sort. Les magistrats qui n'exerçaient que des fonctions d'ordre public étaient élus par le peuple." And he is quite unable on his hypothesis to give any clear explanation of the Council. This is the more to be regretted as the mistake comes from exaggerating the importance of what is within certain limits a most useful suggestion, and one which has thrown much light on an obscure matter.

be elected by lot[1]. I know nothing which makes us feel so clearly our separation from the political world of the Greeks as this. Here is an institution which to us is almost incredible, and yet we find writer after writer assuming that a city cannot be a real democracy without adopting it. The few adverse criticisms on it which have been preserved to us make this only more clear; they are invariably the criticisms of men opposed to democracy, and objection to elections by lot is always accompanied by dislike of democracy. We are told that Socrates used to say that it was foolish to appoint the rulers of the city by lot; no one would have confidence in a pilot or a carpenter or a musician who had been chosen in this way; and yet which had most power to harm, an incompetent magistrate or a bad artist? But then Socrates was an irreconcilable in politics; it was not only election by lot but all the institutions of the city which he criticised; and we know that not only did his objections appear to his contemporaries foolish and pedantic, but his opinions on political matters and the free expression he gave to them were among the reasons why he was put to death as a bad citizen. Socrates thought the lot wrong and foolish; that he did so was a proof of his anti-democratic bias[2].

Even more striking is the attitude of the author

[1] Herod. iii. 80; Plato, Rep. 561 A—B; Aristotle, Rhet. i. 8. Müller-Strübing quotes Isocr. Areop. 20—27 as evidence that the lot was not democratic. On a point of historical fact the witness of Isocrates is of little value; and he is here arguing from the peculiar circumstances of his own time, cf. pp. 96—7; and p. 39.

[2] Xen. Mem. i. 2, 9.

of the pamphlet " On the Constitution of the Athenians[1]." He is a vigorous and confident oligarch:
for him life in a democratic state is scarcely worth
living; his ideal is that the nobles ($oi \, \chi\rho\eta\sigma\tau oi$) should
rule: that the people should be their subjects, their
slaves ($\delta o\hat{\upsilon}\lambda oi$)[2]. All the institutions of Athens,
election by lot included, are in his opinion causes
of unendurable license and disorder. And yet he
cannot refrain from expressing his admiration of the
Athenian constitution, for he acknowledges that it
completely secures what is desired; it is democracy
and therefore hateful to him and to every other right-
minded man who loves order and good government;
but it is at least a successful democracy[3]; it is
impossible to get a more perfect democracy than the
Athenian; the people know what they want and
they have got it; election by lot, freedom of speech,
offices open to all however ignorant and however
uneducated—they are perfectly right he says when
they regard these as an essential part of a democracy.
He too is of opinion that democracy without its
extravagances would be no democracy at all[4].

And this opinion was not peculiar to literary
men, to philosophers and historians; it was the
principle on which the practical men in Greece

---

[1] $'A\theta\eta\nu\alpha i\omega\nu$ $\pi o\lambda\iota\tau\epsilon i\alpha$, formerly attributed to Xenophon. Cf.
esp. i. 9, $\epsilon\dot{\upsilon}\nu o\mu i\alpha$ cannot be found in a democracy; ii. 20, no good
man can live $\dot{\epsilon}\nu$ $\delta\eta\mu o\kappa\rho\alpha\tau o\upsilon\mu\dot{\epsilon}\nu\eta$ $\pi\dot{o}\lambda\epsilon\iota$.

[2] i. 9, $\dot{\alpha}\pi\dot{o}$ $\tauo\dot{\upsilon}\tau\omega\nu$ $\tauo i\nu\upsilon\nu$ $\tau\hat{\omega}\nu$ $\dot{\alpha}\gamma\alpha\theta\hat{\omega}\nu$ $\tau\dot{\alpha}\chi\iota\sigma\tau'$ $\ddot{\alpha}\nu$ $\dot{o}$ $\delta\hat{\eta}\mu o\varsigma$ $\epsilon i\varsigma$
$\delta o\upsilon\lambda\epsilon i\alpha\nu$ $\kappa\alpha\tau\alpha\pi\dot{\epsilon}\sigma o\iota$.

[3] ii. 20, $\delta\eta\mu o\kappa\rho\alpha\tau i\alpha\nu$ δ' $\dot{\epsilon}\gamma\dot{\omega}$ $\mu\dot{\epsilon}\nu$ $\alpha\dot{\upsilon}\tau\hat{\omega}$ $\tau\hat{\omega}$ $\delta\dot{\eta}\mu\omega$ $\sigma\upsilon\gamma\gamma\iota\gamma\nu\dot{\omega}\sigma\kappa\omega\cdot$
$\alpha\dot{\upsilon}\tau\dot{o}\nu$ $\mu\dot{\epsilon}\nu$ $\gamma\dot{\alpha}\rho$ $\epsilon\hat{\upsilon}$ $\pi o\iota\epsilon\hat{\iota}\nu$ $\pi\alpha\nu\tau\dot{\iota}$ $\sigma\upsilon\gamma\gamma\nu\dot{\omega}\mu\eta$ $\dot{\epsilon}\sigma\tau i\nu$.

[4] ii. 19; i. 1—8.

acted. Our knowledge of the internal constitutions of other states besides Athens is small, but it is sufficient to show us that when a state took a democratic constitution election by lot was introduced along with other changes. We are specially told that this was the case at Syracuse[1] and at Tarentum[2]; and when Athens obliged her allies to adopt a democratic form of government, election by lot was as a matter of course included[3].   †

Aristotle's account of the matter is very instructive[4]: he generally speaks of " election " ($\chi\epsilon\iota\rho\sigma\tau\sigma\nu\iota\alpha$, $\alpha\iota\rho\epsilon\sigma\iota\varsigma$) as either aristocratic or oligarchic ; for it gives influence to birth money or ability; he recognises indeed that election by all the citizens is to some extent democratic, but he regards it as a characteristic of the old moderate democracy ($\pi\alpha\tau\rho\iota\alpha$ $\delta\eta\mu\sigma\kappa\rho\alpha\tau\iota\alpha$) and he contrasts this with the new ($\nu\epsilon\omega\tau\alpha\tau\eta$ $\delta\eta\mu\sigma\kappa\rho\alpha\tau\iota\alpha$) where offices are filled by lot[5]. Popular election is that moderate concession to democracy which is desirable in order to give the state permanence by interesting all classes in the government, but he consistently represents election by lot as a sign of what he calls the extreme democracy.

On this point there can be no doubt: election by lot was regarded by those who had experience of it as essentially democratic: if this is the case we may *Objections to this considered.*

---

[1] Diodorus, xiii. 34.

[2] Ar. Pol. vii. 5 (quoted by Gilbert, Gr. St. II. p. 245, n. 1).

[3] C. I. A. i. 9.

[4] Pol. ii. 11, 1273ᵃ; vi. 9, 1294ᵇ; vii. 2, 1317ᵇ; vii. 2, 1318ᵃ.

[5] Pol. viii. 5, 1305ᵃ.

add, it was democratic. It would require some very strong proofs to justify us in putting aside the almost unanimous verdict of the Greeks themselves on a point on which they had complete experience and of which we have no knowledge except what we gain from them.

When then a modern historian[1] informs us that election by lot was not a democratic but an oligarchic institution, and that it was introduced at Athens not to strengthen the democracy but to temper it and make it less repugnant to the defeated oligarchs, we look for some very weighty reasons to justify the paradox. The paradox has been stated lately and has met with a certain amount of favour. This is partly due to the interest which any novelty must arouse in a subject which has been so thoroughly discussed as Athenian constitutional history; a new theory however paradoxical is sure to command a hearing if promulgated with sufficient confidence and at sufficient length; a boldly stated novelty will attract the reader who is wearied with the study of innumerable discussions of minute details. But this favourable reception is also due to the fact that it has no rival: historians have recognised that as a matter of fact election by lot was democratic, but they have not clearly explained the reason why it was so. Generally speaking it seems clear that if any one could be elected to any office, and if the poorest and most ignorant citizen had an equal chance with an Alcmæonid or a pupil of

[1] Müller-Strübing, Aristophanes und die historische Kritik, p. 206 etc.

Gorgias, the state where this was the case was not an aristocracy; but still the necessity and the advantage of the system are not obvious; the orthodox traditional view is vague and has no firm foundation, so that one is naturally tempted to say there is something in the new theory: and many who do not accept it as a whole have altered their statement of the older view, and tell us that, although the lot was of course democratic, yet it was after all to a certain extent aristocratic too[1].

Our object must be then to try and understand not only why election by lot was democratic, but why the ancients considered it essential to a complete democracy.

In order to do so, it will be necessary to recall *What the* certain peculiarities of ancient democracy, which it *Greeks meant* is easy for us to ignore. The fact that the word *by Demo-* "democracy" is still in constant use among us, and *cracy.* that we apply it to political phenomena of the present day, is a great obstacle to our understanding of Greek History. The danger is the greater that the modern use of the word is so nearly akin to the original meaning; but none the less the word has not now the same connotation as it had 2000 years ago;

[1] I do not mean to deny that the lot was often used in states which were not democratic, and that in the period before the Persian wars it was introduced in many oligarchies. As will be seen below, I believe that it was. All I wish to make clear is that, as used at Athens from the time of Persian wars, it was of the very essence of the democracy. The importance of the experiment at Athens caused the older use in oligarchic states to be forgotten just as it destroyed the religious significance. Cf. Curtius, Griechische Geschichte, i. 377 (3rd edition). [Cf. Appendix.]

H. 2

and it requires the greatest care when we are dealing with Greek history and reading Greek books to keep our minds free from modern associations, and to preserve the idea which we connect with the word as pure simple and clearly defined as was that of the Greeks. We have a double difficulty to surmount in achieving this, for not only do we use Greek words when we speak of modern politics, but also our method of education tempts us to think of modern events under Greek forms. Our first acquaintance with political thought comes through Thucydides and Aristotle, and we try to fit the wisdom we have learnt from them to the facts of modern life. By so doing we not only lose the freedom of thought necessary to comprehend new facts, but we unconsciously spoil our apprehensions of Greek life. By trusting too much to the fancied analogies of modern times we lose in the vividness and niceness of our conceptions of ancient politics[1].

The assumption which in one form or another seems to me to underlie most of the difficulties which historians discover in understanding why the *lot* is democratic, depends on a confusion of this kind.

---

[1] Müller-Strübing is one of the worst offenders. He tries (p. 205) to show that at Athens noble birth would have had no influence on elections to administrative posts, because the Radical party at Berlin returned all their candidates at the general election to the North German Parliament in 1867, and even Moltke was not successful when he became a candidate in 1871. Yet the fundamental point is ignored that the Germans elect a legislative assembly, the Athenians generals and judges; in consequence elections in Germany are purely party matters, at Athens they were much more personal.

We naturally feel a desire to fill up the parts of
Athenian history where our direct authorities fail
us ; and as the internal working of the constitution,
which is of all points the most interesting to us, is
that on which we have the least direct information, much ingenuity has been expended in putting
together a whole from the small fragments of certain
knowledge which have been preserved. In this
praiseworthy endeavour, however, many writers have
been influenced by a tacit comparison with modern
societies. The result is much as if an architect tried
to work the fragments of a Greek Temple into a
Gothic Church.

The point in which the process is most misleading *Elections*
is that of elections. We find constantly mentioned *at Athens.*
in Greek history two parties, the Oligarchs and the
Democrats : the " good," the " many:" and we know
that in modern states where popular government prevails there are always two or more parties continually
striving for the chief power in the state, and that
the crises of the struggle are always the periodical
elections. Hence the conclusion is drawn that at
Athens also, where (as we know) there were periodical elections, these were as with us the centre of
political interest, and that by the result of them the
policy of the state was determined; and modern
work on the Athenian constitution has been directed
on these lines, so that all writers even if they have
not paid special attention to the subject assume the
existence of party elections with party organisations
to manage them. So long as we believe this, it is of
course impossible not to be puzzled by the use of

2—2

the lot. It would obviously diminish the power of the popular party, who in Athens at any rate were decidedly in the majority. By losing control over the elections it appears as though they deprived themselves of their chief weapon against their opponents.

Herr Müller-Strübing has ingeniously seized on this point and boldly carried it out to its logical conclusions[1]. It leads him to the paradox that the lot was introduced as a means of moderating the democracy and allowing to the nobles a possibility of attaining office. If however we examine the assumption on which it is based we are met by considerable difficulties. It would seem that, if elections were fought on party lines, and if their result had a serious influence on the direction of the policy, we should be able to find some one or more offices which were filled by the heads of the party, who in consequence of their election would be for a period the recognised leaders of the state. Many such attempts have been made; but they hardly seem to have been successful. Müller-Strübing[2] tries to show

[1] p. 206. That there may be no doubt as to his meaning, he puts the position in the form of a thesis :—

"Die Einführung des Looses bei der Besetzung der Aemter war ein Zugeständniss an die Minorität, war eine Massregel zur Befriedigung der staatsbürgerlichen Bedürfnisse und zur Gewähr-leistung der Rechte der Minorität "

and he then explains how the Athenian Demos is deserving of the highest honour because it never, even in the times of greatest bitterness against the Oligarchs, recalled this concession.

[2] Op. cit. p. 192. "Care was taken that the whole population of the country should at regularly recurring intervals decide on the principles according to which the state should be governed. Just as in modern constitutional states an appeal to the people must

that it was in the chief finance minister that we must look for the prime minister, but he has thereby introduced in the fifth century an office which was probably not instituted till the middle of the fourth[1]. The board of generals are a more usual resource. The high position which they held and the important duties which they had to perform make it reasonable to suppose that if any office was the centre of a party contest it was this, and that if any elections decided the policy of the state it must have been the election of the generals.

Several able writers have spent much ingenuity *The* in explaining the history of Athens on this hypo- *στρατηγοί.* thesis. They point out truly enough that the board of generals were much the most powerful body in the state beside the Assembly and Council. They show that in the fifth century nearly every distinguished statesman was at some time or other a member of this board, and they also bring many facts and many arguments to prove that a man was more likely to be elected at a time when he was popular than when he was not. Pericles was year after year elected general; the time came when his influence was gone; he fell; he was not re-elected. †
The people could in no way better show their

take place at regular periods, when the lawfully regulated time has come for the parliamentary powers to expire. At Athens this appeal to the people took place at the quadrennial election to the more important and influential offices."

[1] His view is the same as that of Boeckh (St. d. Ath. i. 201 (222)), but all later investigations point conclusively to the fact that this office was not created till the time of Eubulus. Cf. infra, pp. 111—3, n. 1.

confidence in a man than by making him their general.

And so the conclusion is drawn that the board of generals had a position like that of our "ministry." They were the "government" for the year. The party to which they belonged had in their hands the executive power; for a year their policy would prevail. As a result it was the election of the generals which was the annual trial of strength between the two parties. It was then that the opposing factions met in an organised conflict. The victory in this carried with it a right to the government of the state for a whole year[1].

+ πρύτανις
τῶν
στρατηγῶν.

I do not propose in this place to discuss all the difficulties which are involved in this theory; difficulties which to a great extent are connected with our ignorance as to the mode in which generals were elected. It will be sufficient to point out that they are so great that some writers have found themselves obliged to assume the existence of an official whom they call πρύτανις τῶν στρατηγῶν. While the other generals were elected each by one of the tribes, this president of the generals was, we are told, elected by the whole people; his power and influence were supreme in the board, and it was by his election that the policy of the year was determined.

Now of course among the στρατηγοί there must always have been one who presided at meetings and could act as representative of the whole board. It is possible that he was called πρύτανις τῶν στρα-

[1] Beloch, Att. Politik, who is followed by Whibley, Political Parties at Athens, p. 121 etc.

τηγῶν, though I believe there is no authority for the expression. But that he was specially elected by the people to the office and not selected by the other generals, or that he was elected by a different constituency to the other generals, cannot be supported by any certain evidence. It is not even clear that the same man was πρύτανις during a whole year. Different again is the στρατηγὸς αὐτοκράτωρ. In time of war, whether the war was in Attica or elsewhere, the Assembly appointed one or more of the generals commander of the detachment of forces which was engaged, and of these in such cases one was often made "commander in chief;" he on such an occasion, either alone or with his colleagues, received special powers; he was, as it was called, made στρατηγὸς αὐτοκράτωρ. But this power belonged to the selected general in virtue of a responsibility which was purely military; it had nothing to do with political influence[1].

It appears then that the supposed necessity of finding some influential office to which the leading men in the state could be periodically elected leads to great difficulties. Three suggestions have been made by those interested in the discovery of the required office, namely, the ταμίας τῶν κοινῶν προσό-δων, the board of generals, and the πρύτανις τῶν στρατηγῶν or στρατηγὸς αὐτοκράτωρ. There is hardly any evidence to support any one of these. And the very uncertainty which exists as to what was

[1] On the election of generals cf. Droysen, in Hermes, ix.; Beloch, Die Attische Politik; Gilbert, Beiträge; Whibley, Political Parties, p. 122, n. 2.

the office, possession of which gave its holder a power in the state equal to that of our prime minister, is sufficient to raise our suspicions as to the truth of the theory of periodical elections which has led scholars on this search.

Elections at Athens not political. I have in fact only referred at all to these theories because it seems as if their very variety were evidence that the basis common to all is unsound. Instead of enquiring whether it was the ταμίας τῶν κοινῶν προσόδων, or the πρύτανις τῶν στρατηγῶν, or the στρατηγὸς αὐτοκράτωρ who was " Prime Minister " at Athens, it would be better perhaps to enquire whether there is any reason for assuming the existence of an elected prime minister at all. All these views come from the supposed necessity of finding some periodical election which determined the course of politics for the ensuing year, or ensuing four years. But the very doubt and uncertainty which prevails as to what office it was which had an importance of this kind perhaps justifies us in doubting whether any such existed.

This uncertainty becomes more important when we realise the absence of any evidence that there were at Athens elections which had the importance attributed to them on this hypothesis; an absence which is perfectly explicable if elections had no political weight, but is quite irreconcilable with a theory which would make them as important as they are in England or America. The negative evidence is irresistible : about the working of the Law Courts, about the debates in the ἐκκλησία and δῆμος, about the military organisation we have a considerable mass of information, but about elections scarcely a word. We have no single reference to a speech made in favour of either party or any candidate at an election, we have no information about the procedure at elections, we do not even know how the voting took place. We cannot account for this silence except on the supposition that elections at Athens had not the importance we are accustomed to assign to them. Were the case otherwise would not Aristophanes have more frequent allusions to them? Would there not be references in the orators? Yet they give no sign that the political conflict was fought out at elections as well as in debates in the ἐκκλησία and before the Law Courts[1].

It is not, I think, saying too much if we conclude that the evidence we possess does not justify us in giving to elections at Athens the importance which the analogy of modern states would lead us to

[1] The most important allusion to electoral procedure in Aristophanes is the scene at the beginning of the Ecclesiazusae, v. 260 etc.—

Cf. esp. 298 ἔπειτα πλησίοι καθεδούμεθ' ὡς ἂν χειροτονῶμεν ἅπανθ' ὁπόσ' ἂν δέῃ τὰς ἡμετέρας φίλας.

Cf. Xen. Mem. iii. 4, 1. Plato Comicus, ap. Kock, fr. 185, λαβοῦ λαβοῦ τῆς χειρὸς ὡς τάχιστά μου, μέλλω στρατηγὸν χειροτονεῖν 'Αγύρριον. Thuc. ii. 65.

Aristotle in the Politics never speaks of elections as party affairs, nor does he refer to party elections connected with them.

On the subject of the election of generals see Droysen, Hermes, ix.

We hear most about the elections of exceptional officials such as ambassadors. A curious fact is preserved about one of these elections. Dem. de corona 149 (277) tells us that Æschines was nominated (προβληθείς) to the office of πυλαγόρας, and elected τριῶν ἢ τεττάρων χειροτονησάντων.

expect. And I propose by a short examination of certain aspects of the Athenian constitution to show why this was so. When this point has been cleared up, we shall be in a better position to understand the Greek view of election by lot.

The reason of this. It was impossible that at Athens elections should have political importance; it was impossible just because Athens was a complete democracy: for the same reason that election by lot was introduced. Elections can only be of political importance when the elected magistrates have for some period considerable independence of action, and when the sovereign power from which they derive their authority is exercised only intermittently. In such cases the people (supposing that the sovereign power and ultimate appeal is with them) does not itself govern the country; it delegates its powers to elected representatives who within wide limits are free *Contrast of ancient and modern democracy.* to do just as they like. Hence the only way which the people have of directing the policy of the state is to elect men pledged to follow certain lines. From this necessity springs inevitably the whole system of party elections. Where the country is governed by an elected assembly, or an elected head of the state, the elections to these offices, in as much as they are almost the only occasions when the people exercises its sovereign power, must be events of the greatest importance.

In a state like Athens just the reverse is the case. It was the essence of the constitution that the demos should itself rule: it did not, as do the people in England or France, appoint its rulers; it did not delegate its power; its sovereignty was not intermittent, it was continually exercised. And in consequence the magistrates at Athens had a position quite other to that held by ministers in a modern democracy. They were not the men to whose wisdom and discretion the votes of the people for a time entrusted the supreme management of affairs: they were appointed to carry out the decrees of the people and to obey its commands. The demos could not bind itself by any election to follow any set policy or to adhere to any plan, for the ἐκκλησία met at least once a month and could at any time be summoned, and at each meeting it was able to discuss and alter the decisions of a previous meeting. Suppose that in any year the στρατηγοί were all chosen from the war party, that these had won at the elections; the people did not thereby deprive themselves of the power of making peace during the year; a popular orator of the opposite party could bring forward a motion and carry it. But if he did so the position of the generals was unaltered; they did not resign, they had simply to carry out the policy of which they disapproved[1]. In England or

[1] Beloch (Att. Politik, p. 15), "Die Geschäfte des Landes aus dem Bema der Pnyx auszuführen war in Athen noch weniger möglich als heute von der Tribune des Parlaments."

This is surely exactly wrong. The object of the whole arrangement of the constitution was to enable orators to guide the business of the state from the Assembly. If he refers to the German Parliament the statement is absurd: a German parliamentary leader has no influence at all on the conduct of business. If the reference is to the English Parliament it is wrong, because the προστάτης τοῦ δήμου had without office just as much power as an English parliamentary leader has with office.

Cf. infra, p. 112 etc.

America the elections are of importance because during the period which follows the people are without any direct control over the fate of the country: they have given their decision, and must abide by it. In Athens, where the sovereign assembly met constantly, the elections had in consequence no political import; men were chosen not for the policy which they advocated but for their ability and character. The question between candidates was always a personal not a party one. An election might be a sign of the popularity and influence of men who supported different policies: it could not bind the people to follow one or the other.

If we remember this, we shall no longer be disturbed by the small number of references to elections which we find in ancient writers, nor wonder at the small place which they filled in the political controversies and passions of the time; and we shall cease to enquire which official held the place of our Prime Minister. And when we realise how this direct sovereignty of the people worked, we shall see why election by lot was considered essential to the maintenance of democracy.

Demo-cracy is inverted monarchy. Sir Henry Maine in his book on Popular Government reminds us that democracy is a form of government, and objects to modern incorrect uses of the word. That the word should have changed its meaning, and should be now used to describe social tendencies is natural and harmless, so long as we recognise the fact; it is however of great importance that we should remember that the Greeks who invented the word did mean by it a definite simple form of government. A Greek had no doubt what he meant by a Democracy; it was a city in which the people gathered together at a definite place in one large visible assembly governed the whole state. When we speak of popular government we mean by "people" a great mass of men living long distances apart from one another who have never seen one another and who never will. The Greeks meant a very limited number of men who were accustomed to come together in a definite place. People with us is a vague idea: the demos to an Athenian was a concrete thing which he had often seen and heard; it was the ἐκκλησία. So too by "government" we mean a vague ill-defined control of the government. In no modern country does the people govern; it is incapable of doing so, it is not sufficiently organised; the work of government is too complicated. Parliament, or Ministers, or the President, govern: the people appoint them and more or less control them. But at Athens the δῆμος did govern. It was not primarily an elective body, that function fell into secondary importance; it was not a legislative body, that was the only duty which was not directly within its sphere; it was a judicial, and above all an executive body.

Sir Henry Maine expresses this by saying that Democracy is inverted Monarchy. In a monarchy the king governs; he has servants, he has advisers; responsible ministers he has none: statesmen are his servants, they do his bidding, they may offer advice, but if their advice be not taken they must be prepared to obey none the less. A favourite may become powerful, but his power depends on the king's favour; there may be rivalry, there may be antagonistic influences; round the bed-chamber of the king, or the salon of his mistress ambitious men contend for the privilege of executing his commands and influencing his will. But great parties there are none, and in a perfect monarchy there are no great ministers: the king himself decides all questions, officials have only to prepare them for his consideration; he has not only the position of a king, but the toil and labour of a ruler.

And so in a perfect democracy the people does all which in a monarchy is the work of the king. All questions of government, all the difficulties of administration, every innovation in every department comes directly before the people: the officials do not decide anything, they only formulate the questions which come before the sovereign people. They do not do the work for the people. They are not appointed to represent it. They are there as clerks or secretaries; their duty is to bring order and arrangement into the mass of details; they help the people to govern, but they help as a freedman helped the Roman Emperor. The people, like the king, has its advisers and favourites, those who know the art of influencing the royal will; these are the orators in the ἐκκλησία, and the first favourite of the time is ὁ προστάτης τοῦ δήμου. But, like the power of the royal favourites, their power does not come from office, and office is not necessary to it; the people, like the king, prefers often to appoint to office men whose advice it would never take; men who do not personally please it, but whose ability and integrity it respects. And as in a perfect monarchy we find no great ministers of state, but the king surrounded by his satellites and courtiers rules alone,—his ministers having no part in the rule, nor any independence of action,—so in a perfect democracy we shall not expect to find great offices; the magistrates will have only to prepare business for the Assembly; they will make ruling easier, but they will not take upon themselves part of the duties of ruling; they will be wheels in the great machine, not separate machines.

Therefore, if the state is to be a democracy, *Results of this.* there must be no powerful officials; for democracy means rule by the demos, government by the ἐκκλησία; and the demos or ἐκκλησία, if it is really to rule, cannot allow any other power to exist in the state, not even if it is a body which derives its authority from the demos. The Greeks themselves were quite clear on this point[1]. They saw well enough that the power of the demos was like that of a monarch, and that a "democracy" could allow no power in the state independent of the Assembly. The "tyrant demos" was a very stern reality to Thucydides and Plato

---

[1] Cf. Aristotle, Pol. viii. (v.) 11, 1313ᵇ—1314 καὶ τὰ περὶ τὴν δημοκρατίαν δὲ γινόμενα τὴν τελευταίαν τυραννικὰ πάντα......, καὶ γὰρ ὁ δῆμος εἶναι βούλεται μόναρχος, διὸ καὶ ὁ κόλαξ παρ᾽ ἀμφοτέροις ἔντιμος, παρὰ μὲν τοῖς δήμοις ὁ δημαγωγός (ἔστι γὰρ ὁ δημαγωγὸς τοῦ δήμου κόλαξ) παρὰ δὲ τοῖς τυράννοις οἱ ταπεινῶς ὁμιλοῦντες, ὅπερ ἐστὶν ἔργον κολακείας. Cf. also iii. 15, 1286ᵃ and vi. (iv.) 4, 1292ᵃ.

and Aristotle. Aristotle clearly recognises that in a democracy all other parts of the state must be made powerless. The demos, just like a tyrant, must prevent any individuals or institutions from acquiring too great power; it can allow neither men nor offices to be independent of itself[1].

Now what the lot did was just that at which Aristotle says the democratic legislator ought to aim. It prevented any individual getting into such a position as to enable him to have power or influence in the state independent of the Assembly. The lot was democratic because so long as officials were elected by it the supremacy of the Assembly was secured. It was introduced not only to prevent rich men being elected (certainly not to give oligarchs a chance of being elected), but to prevent the executive officials being too influential. It was not a δεύτερος πλοῦς to keep down oligarchs, even at the price of getting second-rate men in office; mediocrity in office was its object, because this was the only means of ensuring that not only the name but also the reality of power should be with the Assembly.

Further peculiarities resulting from the nature of elections.
Before however I proceed to analyse the working of it, it will be convenient to add a few words on the general subject of elections, because the peculiarities of the elections at Athens can only be understood by an attention to the results of this principle, that the demos must be supreme.

[1] Ar. Pol. vi. 4, 1292ᵃ ἔτι δ' οἱ ταῖς ἀρχαῖς ἐγκαλοῦντες τὸν δῆμόν φασι δεῖν κρίνειν· ὁ δ' ἀσμένως δέχεται τὴν πρόσκλησιν, ὥστε καταλύονται πᾶσαι αἱ ἀρχαί.

(1) *Political associations.*

The view I have taken of the relation of the "Demos" to party politics is completely supported by what we know of the political associations at Athens. A real party organisation of the modern kind did not exist. There was none of the elaborate system which in modern states gives corporate unity to a party and preserves a continuity of tradition which makes it a permanent settled influence in the state; there was not, so far as we know, any system by which Cleon or Agyrrhius kept a register of the names of their followers and arranged how best to use their votes; there were no public meetings outside the Assembly, and even the private coming together of political friends was looked on with suspicion. Each distinguished man would have a clique or party attached to him; they would profit by his success; when he was influential they would get appointments; when he was unpopular they would be liable to oppression by the courts and the council; but any attempt to organise such associations, to make them permanent and efficient by federating the several cliques, was looked on as contrary to the spirit of the constitution, as "Oligarchic." And so we find that the real leaders of the people, the men who had most influence in the Assembly, depended least on private associations.

The ἑταιρεῖαι at Athens were in fact the re- ἑταιρεῖαι. presentatives in a later stage of society of the *clientèle* which had formerly been attached to great

H.   3

nobles, they were the remnant of a time when the
political interests of the people were confined to the
rivalry of two or more great families; they were
always attached to an individual, nearly always to a
Eupatrid; their members were chiefly young men
closely connected with their leader by birth and
similarity of habits. They were dining clubs, gam-
bling clubs, drinking clubs, and also political clubs;
but they were private and secret; they were small and
short-lived; they represented not a principle but a
person, not a party but a family. It was the great
sign of Antiphon's political sagacity that for a time
he joined these clubs and caused them to work
together for a definite political purpose. By so
doing he was able to overthrow the democracy.

But we cannot understand the strength of the
feeling at Athens against these clubs, nor see why
they should be always looked on as "Oligarchic,"
unless we realise that everything was regarded as
"undemocratic" which gave political influence to
any organisation outside the Assembly, even one
which was avowedly composed of loyal democrats.
The prejudice against party organisations was a
necessary consequence of the principle that the
demos must govern. Had there been well-organised
political clubs they would have withdrawn some of
its importance from the meeting of all the citizens in
the Assembly. There would have been preliminary
meetings, a policy would have been drawn up, men
would have made up their minds how to vote, the
deliberations of the Assembly would have lost something of their reality. Men would have felt that the

question had really been decided elsewhere. Hence, although there was no law against it, there was a reasonable prejudice against any meeting of citizens outside the Assembly. And although of course conferences among leaders must often have taken place, and the immediate friends of any man would come pledged to support him by vote and speech, yet the great mass of those present at a given meeting would come to hear the matter discussed with what is called "an open mind;" they would be free to give their vote according to their own feelings after listening to the speeches on either side. It is possible that an elaborate party organisation would have secured more prolonged deliberation and more security for persistence in any plan; but it would have been undemocratic[1].

(2) *Political importance of the law-courts.*

This peculiar character of the elections may afford a partial explanation of another fact in Athenian History which has been the cause of considerable comment. It is well known that every public man at Athens was liable to constant prosecutions. It is related of Aristophon that he was accused and acquitted 70 times. We know that Pericles Alcibiades Cleophon Callisthenes Demosthenes were all condemned in the courts, and we

Political prosecutions.

[1] Cf. Vischer, Kleine Schriften, vol. i., who collects a number of facts bearing on these ἐταιρεῖαι.

They would give their support to a member whenever he was candidate for an office, but it would be not as a member of a political party but as personal friends; though it is, of course, never possible entirely to separate the two things.

have every reason to suppose that some of them at
least were innocent of the charges brought against
them. Historians have been shocked by this. It
pains us to see the Athenians condemning their
greatest statesmen on a false charge of peculation.
But we ought to remember that this was a necessary
result of the Athenian system of appointment.

In a state where offices are filled by popular
election, personal pique and party prejudice con-
centrate at the elections; it is then that men try to
injure their opponents and help their friends. At
Athens this was not the case. The passions which
with us find expression at elections could there find
no vent except in the law-courts. Popular election
produces the wire-puller: election by lot produces
the sycophant. Political prosecution was the recognised way of injuring an opponent. If we remember
this we shall not feel inclined to attribute the over
litigiousness of the Athenians to pure perverseness of
disposition, and shall be still less disposed to believe
that the statesmen were guilty of all the charges on
which they were accused.

These political trials were really an opportunity
for the expression of popular favour or distrust. A
politician might fail to be elected general, and yet his
eloquence would still enable him to rule the state;
but if he were condemned on a serious charge he
would for the time at least be in disgrace, he would
probably incur partial $\dot{a}\tau\iota\mu\iota a$, he might have to leave
the country, or might even lose his life. And so we
find that every decided change in Athenian policy is
marked, not by the election of a new finance

minister, or a new board of generals, but by the condemnation in the law courts of the former προστάτης τοῦ δήμου.

This was of course only possible because the verdict of the law courts was a direct expression of popular feeling almost as much as was a vote in the Assembly. Accordingly it did not much matter of what a statesman was accused; that which the jurors had to decide was whether the accused still deserved the confidence of the people. Whether an orator were accused of peculation like Pericles, or of ἀστρατία like Cleophon, or of sacrilege like Alcibiades, or of παρανομία like Ctesiphon, his actual guilt or innocence was often a very small part of the issue which depended on the verdict. Such a trial was an opportunity for all enemies of a prominent man to join in procuring his downfall. The accusation was simply an occasion for an attack. The verdict was not on the accusation, it was on the whole life of the man; it was a vote of confidence or non-confidence given by the people as a result of their observation of his political career[1], a vote of the same kind as that which in England is given at a general election.

---

[1] This is illustrated by the fact that bribery was so much more common in the law courts than at elections. Beloch (Att. Politik, p. 144) recognises it when he says of the trial of Timotheos: "Was die Anklage selbst angeht, so war sie juristisch eben so wenig begründet wie sie politisch gerechtfertigt war." He was actually deposed from his office.

Deinarchus (iii. 11) tells the jury to estimate Philocles not by the crimes he had committed, but by those he would have committed had he had the opportunity. This would at any rate be not quite such an immoral doctrine as at first appears, if on

(3) *Good result of absence of party elections.*

This peculiarity of the constitution which to a great extent deprived elections of their importance had one good result. The violence of party conflicts was mitigated, and faction and disorder were thereby discouraged. Athens was free from the danger which must arise when all the party jealousies and passions are concentrated at annually recurring elections. Not only was the danger entirely averted in the appointment to the greater number of offices, since they were filled by lot; but even in the election of generals, and what few other exceptions there were to the rule, the results of the system are seen.

This result was so obviously beneficial that some have considered it alone sufficient to explain and justify the use of the lot; in fact in some Greek states the lot was, we are told, simply used as a means of securing internal peace[1], and it is even possible that this was one of the chief reasons of its use at Athens in the earlier days before the establishment of the democracy[2]. For this result was rightly considered as essential to the integrity and permanence of the democracy, because, as I have pointed out, the existence of στάσις, of violent compact parties,

the result of the trial depended the political power of the accused, and it was not simply a question of punishing him for what he had done.

[1] Ar. Pol. viii. (v.) 3, 1303ª. At Heræa it was introduced for this reason.†

[2] It is an exaggeration however to say, as Lugebil does, that this was the chief object of its later use at Athens.

was an interference with the full independence of
the sovereign Assembly. It remains however true
that the prime reason for the maintenance of the
lot was that, so long as offices were filled by it, the
full supremacy of the Assembly over Council and
administration was secured. I propose now, by
examining the working of the different offices, to
illustrate and corroborate this principle; and to discuss to what extent it was found compatible with
good government and efficient administration.

Additional note on p. 16. †

[Müller-Strübing, p. 208, supports his theory by a
reference to Isocrates, Areopagiticus 20—27. With
reference to this it is only necessary to point out :—

(1) It is not clear whether Isocrates means that
"in the times of Solon and Cleisthenes" they did
not use the lot at all, or only that they used the lot
to decide the claims of selected candidates.

οὐκ ἐξ ἁπάντων τὰς ἀρχὰς κληροῦντες ἀλλὰ τοὺς
βελτίστους καὶ τοὺς ἱκανωτάτους ἐφ᾽ ἕκαστον τῶν
ἔργων προκρίνοντες. [See Appendix.]

(2) That when Isocrates says the old constitution
was more democratic (δημοτικωτέρα) he gives a reason
which is obviously derived from the peculiar circumstances of the time when he is writing and not of
the time of "Solon and Cleisthenes." For the whole
speech of which this passage is a part is a rhetorical
exercise on the faults of modern Athens. And the
allusions are thrown in without any care for their
historical accuracy.

(3) § 17. He simply uses δημοτικωτέρα as synonymous with that which is profitable to the city. He says the true democracy is that which is just and wise.

(4) That even if Isocrates did mean what he said and professed to be writing history and not a political pamphlet, his opinion would be of no value as against the testimony of Herodotus and Plato and Aristotle.]

CHAPTER II.

THE COUNCIL.

THE maintenance of the democracy depended on the condition that there should be no other body in the state which, owing to wealth position birth, or reputation, could act independently of the Assembly. The Greeks saw clearly that power gained by one department must be at the expense of another. There was nothing to which they attached so much importance as the preservation of a due balance of power between the various institutions. This is shown in the dread of men of conspicuous ability which was so common. But in a democracy the true balance, or proportion in the government was that the Assembly should have all the power: anything which could interfere with it was a distortion[1]. It was as much the object of a good democrat to

---

[1] That is in administration. The theory of Greek constitutional law was that the Assembly should be free only within the limits of the laws; these were normally unchangeable (cf. Wilamowitz-Möllendorff, *Aus Kydathen*); legislation was not one of the regular functions of the people. But (this always excepted) in a true democracy its power would not be impeded by the competition of any other legally constituted body.

weaken all other assemblies and institutions as it
was of a tyrant to kill all other able men. And
this is what the lot did at Athens[1].

For any state which is not governed by an assembly of all the citizens must be governed either
by a smaller council, or by one or more magistrates.
This the Greeks saw clearly enough, just as they saw
that the power of one of these organs depended on
the weakness of the others. They themselves divided the city states into three classes: Monarchy,
Aristocracy or Oligarchy, Democracy; and to these
added the state with a mixed constitution—the
πολιτεία as Aristotle calls it. In all of these we
find existing more or less developed the three organs
of government, the ἐκκλησία or great assembly of
citizens; the βουλή or senate, a smaller select council;
and the executive magistrates. The power was
divided among these three, and what was gained by
one was lost by another; and just as a Democracy
was a state where the ἐκκλησία maintained its
power and held the government in its own hands,
so in an Aristocracy or Oligarchy we find the chief
power held by the βουλή or smaller council. It
would be equally correct if we substituted for the
Greek words, "Rule of the Many," "Rule of the Few,"
the expressions, "Rule by the Assembly," "Rule by
the Council." To preserve the Democracy it was
necessary to keep up the power of the ἐκκλησία as

---

[1] Aristotle expressly tells us that in a democracy all other
offices (ἀρχαί) will lose power : τέταρτος δὲ τρόπος τὸ πάντας περὶ
πάντων βουλεύεσθαι συνιόντας, τὰς δ' ἀρχὰς περὶ μηθενὸς κρίνειν
ἀλλὰ μόνον προανακρίνειν. Pol. vi. (iv.) 4, 1298ᵃ.

against that of the βουλή and the magistrates; and this is what the lot did.

Of course it seldom happened that there was a state where any form of government was quite perfect. Even a complete monarchy, where the executive ruler was quite independent and irresponsible, was rare; though the Greek states under the tyrants had had some experience of such an arrangement. But this was a passing phase, and Athens had never fallen under the despotism of a constitutionally appointed executive body as Sparta to some extent had, and the danger of this does not seem at the beginning of the fifth century to have been great. There was no tyrant, the continuation of whose rule interfered with the independence of the assembly: the more pressing danger to be met by those who wished to establish a democracy was the rule of the aristocratic council; for it was round a council that the power of the old nobles had centred.

The power of this council is the most striking *The council in the city state.* fact in the history of all city states; in mediæval Germany and in Italy just as much as in all the ancient cities, Greek Latin and Phœnician, which were scattered round the shores of the Mediterranean. It does not matter whether a seat in the council be hereditary, whether the appointment be by cooptation, or even by direct or indirect popular election; with the council rests the real power of the state, and to become a senator is the object of ambition for all who themselves aim at power. It is the councillors, the senators, the *rathsherrn* who

are looked up to by their fellow-citizens as their
rulers; it is they who have a monopoly of the
distinctions and rewards of government; it is on
their decision that the welfare of the town depends;
to be one of them is to be admitted to the *arcana*
of government. There may be a sovereign popular
assembly to which certain rights are reserved; but
its power is uncertain and its practical importance
small, compared with that of the council. And
though there are of course magistrates with special
duties who have a formal precedency over all other
members of the council, yet as a matter of fact we
generally find that the magistrates have little independence. They act not as individuals, but as
members of the greater body to which they belong;
the man who is consul or *bürgermeister* for a year
is hardly distinguished from his associates in the
council who have held office or will succeed him in
it. When the common man meets a senator or
councilman in the street, he looks on him with the
respect or envy which is due to one who has by his
office an authority which no ability nor experience
can counterbalance; he is before one who is politi-
cally his better. Whether the council is filled by
men of good birth and great wealth, or whether men
are elected to it for their merit, those who belong to
it are an exclusive body; they are a ruling clique
within the state; between them and all other citizens
there is a great gulf fixed.

The government in an Aristocratic or Oligarchic
state is then government by a council: and all
experience shows that a small body is likely to get

into its hands more power than legally belongs to it.
But a council of some kind is necessary. A large
assembly of many thousands cannot alone govern a
state. The problem of ancient democracy was therefore to find a form of council which would help the
assembly in the work of government, but would not
usurp further power. There must be a council
which would be efficient, but not exclusive; which
would help the ἐκκλησία, but not lead or oppose it.

Now at Athens there had been in the old days
an aristocratic government which was centred round
a council. The founders of the Athenian democracy
had therefore a double task: they had to destroy,
and to build up. They had to take away the power
of the old council, and invent a new one which would
do the work without making for itself an independent place. For both tasks they used the same
instrument, election by lot. By it they broke down
the influence of the old council, and by it they made
a new one which answered all the requirements of a
complete democracy.

Our knowledge of the history of the change is
unfortunately very small; for the most important
facts we are reduced to guess-work: we have therefore to be content with relating what happened.
How events happened, what brought them about,
what the immediate causes were, we cannot know.

(1) How election by lot was used to deprive *The
Areopagus.*
the old aristocratic council of its power is so well
known that I need not dwell on the subject. Grote
has pointed out how when once it was decided that
the Areopagus should consist of all ex-archons, and

that the archons should be chosen by lot from all citizens[1], the power and influence of the Council of the Areopagus was gone[2]. Some religious mystery still attended it, its meetings still had some of the dignity which comes from old associations, but its political importance was over, and it remained a harmless and picturesque relic to tell of a past which was gone for ever.

Whatever may have been the time and occasion of this reform, there is no doubt that the object and the result of causing the Archons,—and so, indirectly, the members of the Council of the Areopagus,—to be elected by lot from all the citizens, was once for all to do away with the influence of the old nobility, and give the new institutions free play. Most investigations into the subject do not go further than this point. I propose now to proceed to examine how election by lot was used in the creation of the new democracy; for it might easily have happened that at Athens the old *régime* was succeeded as at Rome by a new aristocracy, or by a mixed constitution. That this did not happen was due above all to the fact that the new offices were in most cases filled by lot.

The Council of 500.   (2) Just as the centre of the old constitution was the Council of the Areopagus, so the key to the new system is to be found in the Council of 500. We are told that this was instituted by Solon as the Council of 400[2], and enlarged by Cleisthenes to 500;

---

[1] I reserve a discussion on the question when the lot was introduced for election of archons. Cf. infra, p. 78 etc.

[2] [See the Appendix for the new light lately thrown on this.]

but we have no further knowledge of it in the pre-Periclean period; we do not know what it did, nor how it was filled; we do not know why Solon founded it, nor whether Cleisthenes enlarged its powers. There is scarcely a single mention of it until the time when we find it in the complete democracy existing as the great committee of the assembly, through which nearly all business had to pass[1]. Without attempting to reconstruct its previous history we must be content to show what were the peculiarities which distinguished it from similar bodies in other states, and how these were connected with the manner in which its members were chosen.

A council of some kind there must be. However much power was given to the assembly, and however active it was, it was obviously impossible that it should alone transact all the work of government. The problem was to find some form of council which would be strong enough to relieve the assembly of the multitudinous details of business, and yet would not gather round itself authority, or influence, so as to become in any way independent of the assembly. A council of men elected for life was of course out of the question; it would have been merely the Areopagus again under a new form. But there were grave objections against having a council filled by popular election at all. For, firstly, the influence of the nobles was still so great that they would un-

---

[1] Unless it is referred to in Herodotus, v. 72; ix. 5. There seems no proof of the supposition of Fustel de Coulanges that the council was appointed by lot because the original duty of the Prytanies was care of the sacred fire. (La Cité antique, p. 390.)

doubtedly have occupied nearly all the places. Owners of nearly all the land, the inheritors of all the traditions of the state, hereditary priests, judges, generals, statesmen, they still had an influence which would have been little weakened by popular election. And, secondly, there was another reason why any council elected by the people would fail to do what was required, even if the influence of the nobles were broken. It would inevitably be too good. The power of any assembly does not depend only on the privileges given it by law, but on the character and antecedents of the men who form it. Had there been at Athens a council elected (even if annually elected), though its duties had been nominally exactly the same as those of the Council of 500, it would constantly have gained in power at the expense of the Assembly. The smaller a body the better it works. If in a state there are two bodies, one of many thousands meeting four times a month, another say of a hundred meeting daily, whose members are chosen from all their fellow-citizens, at the end of a hundred years the whole business will really be transacted in the smaller body, and the larger will have little to do but to ratify the decrees passed by it. And, in consequence, any citizen who is not a member of the smaller body will be in a position of disadvantage; he will be without the influence and experience which only councillors possess. The government may be a very good government; it will be what Aristotle would have held to be the best; but it will not be a democracy; it will not be government by the Assembly.

The requirements at first seem impossible; a council which shall be efficient and strong but shall never acquire independent authority; a council which shall do the work for the assembly and never put itself in opposition to the assembly. The Athenian solution was as simple as it was ingenious. The council is there to do the work which the assembly has not time to do, work which the assembly would do if there were not so much of it; but if the work of the council is of the same kind as the work of the assembly it can be done by the same people. The work of the assembly is done by all Athenian citizens together, the work of the council shall be done by all Athenian citizens in rotation. 500 one year shall be selected by lot; when they have had their term of office they shall select again by lot 500 to succeed them. In this way the council will be an exact image of the ἐκκλησία. We shall gain additional working power, and we shall not create an unruly servant.

The great point of this invention was that it *Method of* gave practically to nearly every Athenian citizen a *appoint-* *ment.* seat on the council. Men were eligible to the council so soon as they reached the age of thirty; the number of Athenian citizens above the age of seventeen was at the greatest not more than about 30,000, and about 460 B.C. it was probably much smaller than this. A simple calculation will show that, unless re-election was frequent, considerably more than half the citizens must at some period of their life have been members of the council. If with some authorities we reckon the number of citizens at from 15,000 to 20,000,

there would not have been enough citizens to fill the
council without re-election[1].

The enormous importance of this will be evident
at once. It made all the difference whether any
citizen might be elected, or whether nearly every
citizen must be elected[2]. We can well understand
how anyone who had had experience of it would
look on election by lot as essential to a democracy.
Most important among the results would be its
educational value. In speaking of the Oligarchic
council I remarked how much the influence it had was
due to the fact that its members had a monopoly of
certain kinds of experience. They alone understood
the secret ways of statesmanship; they were behind
the scenes; they had experience which if not so
peculiar as that of a cabinet minister is greater than
that of a member of Parliament. Now of course the
Athenian council was not such a good school of
politics as the Roman senate; but still it was before
the council that the government of the city day by

[1] For the population of Attica cf. Boeckh, Staatshaushaltung,
i. p. 42, etc.; Beloch, Zur Bevölkerungslehre; Thuc. ii. 13.
According to his account of the number of Athenians available for
military service, the total number of citizens above 17 years of
age must have been about 30,000. Dem. Aristogeiton, 51, puts
the population lower, εἰσί που δισμύριοι πάντες Ἀθηναῖοι.

I do not know that we have any means of finding the average
length of life at Athens, so that we must be content to say that
when the population was at its highest the number of citizens
who reached the age of 30 each year must have been something
less than 1000.

[2] On the question of re-election to the council cf. infra, p. 56.
Although it was possible and sometimes occurred, what evidence
there is seems to show that it was not frequent.

day passed, its members were directly responsible for
the safety of the city, they had to interview foreign
ambassadors, they had often in private session to
receive information concerning the welfare of the
city. Membership of the council thus gave a
practical insight into all that went on in Athens,
and it must have been of the very greatest importance that this practical experience was not confined
to a few but that every one had an equal share in it.
Professor Freeman has remarked with justice on the
political experience possessed by an average Athenian citizen; but if he had only sat in the Assembly,
it would have lost much of its value; if he had
never sat in the council, if none of his relatives had
ever done so, if he had never spoken familiarly to
anyone who had been a councillor, his experience,
although considerable, would yet have been one-sided
and imperfect.

The principle of rotation is even more strikingly
illustrated if we look at the internal arrangements of
the council. As the council was to the Assembly
so were the πρυτάνεις to the council. The council
was a committee of the assembly, to which each
member was appointed in rotation; its duty was to
clear the ground for the action of the assembly by
disposing of and arranging all the details. The
Prytanies were a committee of the council on which
each member served in turn; it was a permanent
sub-committee in almost permanent session; but
the members of it continually changed, and thus by
means of it the council was able to transact a mass
of business without unduly taxing the energies of

4—2

any individual member. And if we pass from the Prytanies to the ἐπιστάτης[1] we find the same system of rotation carried even further. For one day of the year, if not every councillor, at least the great majority of them were in turn formal presidents of the whole state. In turn each presided in the meetings of the council, and (if there happened to be one on that day) of the assembly; he took the chief place in any public dinner in the Prytaneum; he took the first place in any public procession; he had the key of the state treasury. Could equality, could democracy go further?

Were the leading politicians members? There can, I think, be no doubt that election by lot was a democratic institution, but the original difficulty with which we started is not yet solved. How was it possible to govern the city even passably with such a constitution? What after all had this council to do, and how did it do it? It is difficult not to believe that if the council was really an important body, and if the government of the state was really managed by it, the leading men and great politicians must in some way have become members. The influence which would belong to membership is just what an ambitious man would prize; a seat must have been an object of desire; and it would surely be of great importance that a body on which such responsibilities rested should number among its members men with special knowledge of affairs, and men who in virtue of their well-known character and position would feel their

[1] The change made in the arrangements in the 4th century does not materially affect this point.

responsibility, and exercise more discretion than would men of no experience. Nothing is so dangerous as a body entrusted with public duties, the members of which have not learnt the caution which comes from experience.

It has therefore been generally assumed that in some way or another leading politicians did manage frequently to get a seat in the council; and that the popular orators of the time were as conspicuous in the debates of the council as in those of the larger assembly.

There is however some difficulty in understanding †how this was possible; a difficulty which is much increased by our ignorance of the manner in which the election was managed. If, as is generally held, the lots were drawn only among the men who were nominated or came forward as candidates, then of course by constantly coming forward, any single individual would be able to ensure a considerable probability that he would be not unfrequently among those chosen. But even this point is uncertain[1].

[1] The only passage which I know as directly bearing on it is Lysias, xxxi. 33, where speaking of a man who had been elected a senator the orator says, προθυμῶς κληρωσόμενος ἦλθε. Making allowance for the desire of a rhetorical contrast, these words at the most do not imply more than that Philo had taken care that his name was entered on the lists of those eligible to the council. Such a list there must have been. If anyone's name was omitted he would claim to have it put on. The justice of his claim would not be tried unless he were actually chosen. In the parallel speech, pro Mantitheo, of Lysias, there is no reference to any special candidature. The fact also that Socrates was once a member of the council is evidence that the lots were not drawn only among men who came forward. It is improbable that he at his age would have volun-

It is perhaps equally probable that the election was managed by drawing lots, not among the names of special candidates, but from an official list of all who were eligible and not during that year otherwise occupied on the state service.; this list being made out by demes, and a certain number drawn from each deme.

Was the lot honestly worked?

Some historians have felt the difficulty so strongly that they have supposed there was some underhand means by which a public man might procure his election[1]. The chief support for this is a passage where Æschines refers to Demosthenes as one who had got himself appointed councillor, not by any regular means, but by bribery and intrigue[2]. It is however hardly safe to depend much on a casual accusation of dishonesty brought by Æschines against Demosthenes. Had there been any foundation for

tarily made an exception to his ordinary mode of life, and come forward as candidate for a seat in the council. Neither Xenophon nor Plato says anything which would lead us to suppose that this was the case (Xen. Hist. i. 7, 15; Plato, Apol. 32). [See Appendix.]

[1] Gilbert (Beiträge, p. 80 etc.) suggests that there was some way of getting elected as substitute (ἐπιλαχών) to another man, and then getting him ejected on δοκιμασία. There is absolutely no evidence for this, for the passage quoted from Plato Comicus (ap. Meineke, 2, 670) tells us nothing.†

[2] Æschines in Ctesiphontem, 62, οὐδὲ λαχὼν οὐδὲ ἐπιλαχὼν ἀλλ' ἐκ παρασκευῆς πριάμενος, and again ib. 73, βουλευτὴς ὢν ἐκ παρασκευῆς.

There is a similar expression used of appointment to a priesthood. Demosthenes in Theocrinem, lviii. 29, καὶ τὴν μὲν ἀρχὴν ἣν ἐκεῖνος ἄρχων ἐτελεύτησεν, ἱεροποιὸς ὤν, παρὰ τοὺς νόμους ἦρχεν οὗτος, οὔτε λαχὼν οὔτ' ἐπιλαχών, and Æschines in Timarchum, 106 (125), οὐκ ἔστιν ἥντινα πώποτ' οὐκ ἦρξεν ἀρχὴν, οὐδεμίαν λαχὼν οὐδὲ χειροτονηθεὶς, ἀλλὰ πάσας παρὰ τοὺς νόμους πριάμενος.

the charge it would hardly have been passed over so lightly. It is probably nothing but a characteristic method of expressing annoyance that Demosthenes had been fortunate enough to get elected.

The reference is, however, of some interest as being one of the clearest cases in which we find that a politician was to some extent helped in his measures by the fact that he was a member of the council. Others do occur, but on the whole hardly with sufficient frequency to justify us in supposing that a seat was necessary for a politician, or that he could in any way reckon upon being a member. It seems as though most well-known men were in the council at least once (though this cannot be proved for nearly all); but, as we must remember, to have a seat once was not more than any citizen might hope for[1].

The only other evidence on the matter comes *Evidence of inscriptions.* from some lists which have been preserved of Prytanies, belonging to the fourth century[2]. Of these three give about the full number of councillors belonging to one tribe. An examination of them gives the following results:

(1) The number of members belonging to each deme appears to vary with the size of the deme, and the number elected for the same deme in different

---

[1] In a great number of cases in which men are mentioned in connection with the council, the man was not necessarily himself a member, but was present either as an official of some kind, or simply as a private man there on business. Cf. Lysias, v. 33. When we are told that Pericles was regular in his attendance at the council, it does not follow that he was a member. He went in his capacity of general.

[2] C. I. A. II. 864 etc.

years seems to be constant. From this we may gather that at the election a certain number were chosen from each deme, and that the members were not chosen from the whole tribe indiscriminately.

† (2) There are a few cases where the names of the same deme are preserved for more than one year. Among these only one case of re-election is to be found. This perhaps shows that re-election was not very frequent.

† (3) No names of distinguished politicians occur; but on the other hand there are a large number of names which can be identified as occurring, (a) in the private speeches of the orators, (β) in lists of trierarchs, (γ) as members of distinguished families. However, a very large proportion of the names are completely unknown, many being names which occur nowhere else in Greek history and must therefore belong to families of no distinction or wealth.

On the whole, so far as we can see, the different strata of Athenian society are each fairly represented. There is no evidence that wealthy and distinguished men abstained from sitting in the council, nor is there a larger number of them in these lists than would be a fair proportion.

(4) It is remarkable that three times near relatives (twice two brothers, and once father and son) sit together. This can hardly be a coincidence.

Leading statesmen not necessarily members. The conclusion from this evidence is that we have no reason for supposing that public men could in any way command a seat in the council, and it would, I think, be difficult to find the record of any events in Athenian history which would justify the assertion that a place in it was necessary to an ambitious man. It was possible to rule the whole state without having a seat in it. How this was so will be seen if we examine more minutely what the duties of the council were[1].

The council was not, as we are apt to think, a *Duties of* † *the council.* dignified deliberative body, where men met together quietly in order to discuss and prepare schemes for the public welfare, which should afterwards be laid before the Assembly and receive its sanction. Had the council had to initiate and decide upon *policy*, the leading orators must have been members of it; and had they been members it would doubtless have acquired this function. But, as it was, its duties though no less important were far less imposing. It was not a deliberative, but an executive body; it was concerned not with policy, but with business. It had to carry out the decrees of the Assembly; it was occupied with innumerable points of detail; it had to make decisions, not on matters of peace and war or internal reforms, but on the appointment of subordinate officials, on the amount of tribute to be paid by some ally, the necessity for rebuilding warehouses, or restoring triremes. Its time was occupied with the inspection of accounts, the making of contracts, the paying of money, the hearing of

[1] If I am right in supposing that the method of appointment prevented the leading politicians sitting regularly in the council, it will also follow that no one else could procure his election or re-election, and therefore that re-election did not prevail to such an extent as to interfere with the truth of the principle which I stated above, pp. 49—50.

petitions from individuals, the reception of information about the position of the enemy's fleet, or the price of corn in the Euxine; in fact, with the innumerable matters of administration which in a modern state are brought before the permanent officials[1]. A reference to its most prominent duties will make this clear.

(1) προβού-λευμα.   The most important of its duties was perhaps the preparation of business for the Assembly; it is well known that no decree could be passed

[1] Cf. [Xenophon] Ἀθηναίων Πολιτεία, iii. 2, etc. for the duties of the council;—the chief are, the appointment of 400 trierarchs every year, the assessment of the tribute every four years, to decide judicial questions, εἴ τις τὴν ναῦν μὴ ἐπισκευάζει ἢ κατοικοδομεῖ τι δημόσιον. It is difficult to understand to what the πολλὰ περὶ νόμων θέσεως in iii. 2 refers.

Boeckh, p. 187 (208), gives an account of the financial activity of the council, which shows well the kind of work it had to do:—

"It had, according to the pamphlet on the Athenian Constitution, to occupy itself with provision of money, with reception of the tribute, and as we can conclude from another source, with other matters connected with the tribute, with the administration of the marine and the sanctuaries; the leasing of the customs was conducted under its supervision, those who had public money or sacred money from the state had to pay it in the presence of the council, or it had to exact payment according to the contracts, so that it was entitled to arrest and imprison the farmers or their sureties and collectors, if they did not pay; in the council chamber the Apodectai gave their report on the receipts and the money which was due; in the presence of the council the treasurers of the goddess handed over and took over the treasure and received the fines; it determined the administration of the money, even in small matters, such as the pay of the poets; we have especial mention of its superintendence over the cavalry which was maintained by the city, and the examination of the invalids who were supported at the public expense, as part of its duties; the public debts are paid under its guidance."

which had not been introduced officially by the council. The object of this rule is simple; it was not desired to give the council a special influence, nor to restrict the freedom of debate in the Assembly; it was not in any way a law which as at Rome gave the magistrates alone the right of introducing business. This rule did not weaken the Assembly, but strengthened it, because it provided for the proper arrangement of debates. The Prytanies summoned the Assembly, and, as the chief committee, the council had to prepare business for it. It was then only natural that they should have notice beforehand of all measures which would be introduced, since they would have to make public the matters to be discussed, and to arrange the order of business.

And, again, anyone who has had experience of public debates will know how difficult it is to get business done, and especially what trouble is caused by inaccuracy in the wording of motions. Now we know that the Athenians were very particular on this point; they took great care to provide that there were no verbal discrepancies in their laws, and no discrepancy between the laws and decrees; it was the duty of the council to see that all motions brought before the Assembly were properly worded. If an orator wished to propose a motion, he had first to move that the council introduce a προβούλευμα on the subject; they had to consider the matter of the proposal he wished to make, and then embody it in a motion in such a way as seemed to them most convenient; in this way provision was made

for a consideration of the form of a Psephism
before the motion itself came before the Assembly.
As a rule the orator would doubtless be consulted
by the council, and if he were a man of position we
may imagine they would propose the προβούλευμα
in the very words which he suggested.

There would be another reason for this law.
When a motion was proposed it would often be difficult to tell at first what would be its result if passed,
and questions would be raised to which the answers
would only be found by special enquiry. This it
would be the duty of the council to make. They as
the centre of the executive government, in constant
communication with all the officers, and with powers
to summon and examine all witnesses, would be able
to collect the evidence to be laid before the Assembly.

This work of the drafting and preparing motions
is really part of the subordinate work of the executive officers, for it is a way of helping to the attainment of an end which is proposed by someone else[1].
The council in doing this was not directing the
state, it was only helping other people to do so, and
giving effect to their wishes[2]. And it is an important confirmation of this view that in the last few
years inscriptions have been discovered from which it

---

[1] The fact that an orator was always held responsible for any
motion proposed by him shows that the council had not power
seriously to alter the matter of a decree, and that in the exercise
of its Probouleutic duties it did not in any way concern itself with
the wisdom of the policy proposed.

[2] This is shown too by Aristotle's distinction between ἡ βουλή
and πρόβουλοι. Cf. infra, p. 74.

appears that there was at Athens a body of men called συγγραφείς whose special duty it was to help ⟨συγγρα-⟩ in drafting decrees[1]. We are not able to say with ⟨φείς.⟩ confidence whether they were members of a permanent bureau, or whether the men were appointed, as in the case of the other exceptional officials, only when their help was specially wanted, but we have the record of their existence and activity in the text of decrees which had been drawn up by them. In these cases, though the draft of the bill, as on all other occasions, was introduced to the Assembly by the Prytanies, the council had not really performed any probouleutic duties at all; they simply brought forward what the συγγραφείς had proposed. We find another instance of a similar procedure in the case where a single individual is commissioned by the Assembly to draw up the text of a decree, and then the council is ordered[2] to bring his proposal before the people.

In matters of foreign policy also the duty of the council was limited to the introduction of a treaty proposed either by Athenians who as ambassadors had been empowered to conduct negociations, or by the ambassadors of other states, or,

---

[1] Cf. Schœll, Commentationes in honorem Mommsennii; Foucart, Bulletin de Correspondance Hellénique, 1880, p. 225; Sauppe, Index lect. Acad. Göttingen, 1880—81; also C. I. A. i. 58; iv. 27ᵇ. They are mentioned before the end of the fifth century.

[2] C. I. A. iv. 27ᵇ, vv. 59—61. περὶ δὲ τοῦ ἐλαίου τῆς ἀπαρχῆς ξυγγράφσας Λάμπων ἐπιδειξάτω τῇ βουλῇ ἐπὶ τῆς ἐνάτης πρυτανείας, ἡ δὲ βουλὴ ἐς τὸν δῆμον ἐξενεγκέτω ἐπάναγκες. The decree of which this is a clause is proposed by Lampon himself.

finally, of proposals made by the council of the allies[1].

It seems then as though the duties of the council in preparing decrees varied greatly. As it had to arrange the order of business in the Assembly, all decrees had to be brought before it for preliminary consideration; but it does not follow that it had full power of discussing and altering them. If, as sometimes was the case, a proposal was to be made of such a nature that exceptional skill and judgement was necessary in drawing up the text, the matter was generally entrusted by the Assembly to an exceptional commission of one or more men. In the case of a large number of motions which were introduced by the enterprise of a single orator, the council would simply adopt the words proposed by the author of the decree, making perhaps such alterations as were necessary to render it formally correct. The decrees introduced by the council on its own initiative would in number probably far

---

[1] C. I. A. ii. 51 = Hicks, Greek H. Ins. 84.

    C. I. A. ii. 57ᵇ =   ,,   ,,   94.

From the year 378 there were present in Athens representatives of all the allied states. They had power to meet and discuss matters which concerned the alliance, but the ultimate decision was always reserved for the Athenian assembly. The council however could ask for their opinion on any matter. In the first of the cases quoted the council asks the allies to consider the matter, and give their opinion to the Assembly. (τοὺς συμμάχους δόγμα ἐξενεγκεῖν εἰς τὸν δῆμον, ὅτι ἂν αὐτοῖς βουλευομένοις δοκῇ ἄριστον εἶναι.) In the second the allies have communicated their opinion to the council, and the council incorporates it in a προβούλευμα. (ἐπειδὴ δὲ οἱ σύμμαχοι δόγμα εἰσήνεγκαν εἰς τὴν βουλὴν δέχεσθαι τὴν συμμαχίαν...καὶ ἡ βουλὴ προυβούλευσεν κατὰ ταῦτά.) Cf. also p. 66.

exceed these other classes, but their separate importance would not be so great. The council would be responsible for all the decrees connected with the ordinary management of the state, constantly recurring votes of money, permission to repair public buildings, grants of citizenship, votes of thanks; matters which required a vote of the Assembly, but which would as a rule be passed without opposition, and often without discussion[1].

In these purely administrative matters the council took the initiative, and its proposals were doubtless generally adopted, for it was the representative of the permanent administrative offices. Had the council been a strong body, one which had a spirit and desires of its own, its Probouleutic duties would have been a danger to the freedom of the Assembly, for the power of initiative not only in subordinate points of administration but in great questions of policy might easily have been lost to the larger body. The Assembly would have existed only to discuss, to adopt, or reject the proposals of the council. It was a result of the method of appointment by lot to the council that this did not happen, and that, while it performed the duties of preparing and arranging business, it did not put any check on the complete freedom of discussion in the Assembly[2].

---

[1] A great number of the decrees which we possess are of this nature, as they record votes of thanks and honours to foreign envoys; they would be part of the ordinary international courtesy, and were naturally proposed by the council on its own authority.

[2] We hear of a board called συλλογείς τοῦ δήμου, but are not

(2) *Administrative duties.*   The administrative duties were so various that we can only take a few typical instances of cases where we are well informed concerning them. The extent of these duties will be more apparent when we come to deal with the other magistrates with whom the council was intimately connected. For my present purpose it is sufficient to point out that the administrative duties of the council were always connected with matters of detail; there is no sign that it could form decisions of any political moment. It could only carry out the policy of the Assembly. This is very clearly shewn by a decree which is preserved to us of the latter part of the 4th century, and is worth quoting.

In 325 B.C. an expedition was to be sent out to carry into execution a plan for settling colonies in the Adriatic. A decree was brought before the people to give the orders necessary to the proper fitting out of the expedition[1]. After various orders to the inspectors of the dockyards, and other officials specially concerned, come the following clauses:—"And the Council of 500 shall superintend the fitting out of the expedition, and punish according to the laws any of the trierarchs who are unruly. And the Prytanies shall provide that the council be in constant session on the quay till the expedition has sailed. And the

told what they had to do. Cf. Boeckh, vol. ii. p. 115 (3rd Ed.); C. I. A. ii. 607, 741, 1174. It is difficult to see what scope there was for the activity of a special board in summoning the Assembly. They are apparently different from an elected officer of the same name mentioned by Harpocration.†

[1] C. I. A. ii. 809 b.

Athenian people shall choose[1] ten men from all the Athenians, and they shall superintend the fitting out of the expedition in the same way as the council is ordered to do. And the council and the Prytanies after superintending the outfit shall be crowned by the people with a golden crown to the value of 1000 drachmas. And if anything is necessary to supplement this decree, the council shall have power to pass a decree, so long as it does not invalidate anything which has been decreed by the people."

This we may consider as the regular form of procedure; it is an excellent illustration of the position which the council held. The Assembly declares for a policy, arranges the general principles on which it shall be carried out, and then leaves the management of all details, within certain limits, to the council. When we are told that the council was responsible for keeping up the number of the triremes, the case is precisely similar; the Assembly made the decree or law which determined the size of the fleet; the council was responsible for its execution.

It was moreover especially the duty of the council *Financial* to watch over the public finances. Of this I shall *Duties.* have more to say later, for, as I shall point out, the management of the finances is more difficult to understand than any other part of the system. It will be sufficient here to recall the fact that the council had no power alone to levy any tax, or spend any

---

[1] That these ἀποστολεῖς, being exceptional officials, should be chosen by popular election is, as I shall afterwards show, in accordance with the invariable custom.

money without authority. What it had to do was to see that the regular taxes were properly collected or sold, and that the money was paid in by the separate officials; to decide questions in disputed cases about the assessment of the tax; and to pay money as required to the various officials.

The council was in financial matters of special importance, and for the following reason. All the money of the state passed through its hands, and it was in constant communication with all the other officials; the control of the finances therefore depended on the information which was to be found either in the council chamber itself, or in the offices of the various boards which were grouped round it. And moreover the council had the duty of calling the attention of the Assembly to any deficit. For as it was responsible for the management of all the various public services, and as these could not be maintained without supplies, if when the officials applied to the council there was no money to give them, the council would have to ask the Assembly for more money; it would have to state what the deficiency was, and would perhaps accompany the statement by a recommendation of some way of raising the sum. There was however no constitutional custom which compelled the Assembly to accept the suggestion made by the council.

Foreign relations. It might be thought that there was one duty of the council which formed an obvious exception to the principle I have laid down. It had to receive foreign envoys, and consider the terms of any treaty or agreement which was to be proposed. This was not however different from other occasions on which it prepared business for the Assembly. The council could not in any way influence the decision of the Assembly; all that it had to do was to learn from the strangers the business on which they had come, the powers which they had, and the terms which they were ready to propose. In accordance with this information a Probouleuma would then be drawn up introducing the subject to the Assembly. In this as in other cases the object of the Probouleuma was not in any way to influence the decision on the question to be debated, but to make clear what that question was. This is abundantly evident from the inscriptions, and in those cases where our other authorities give an account of the reception of ambassadors there is nothing inconsistent with it.

For instance, Thucydides in the 5th book[1] gives an account of the reception of a Spartan embassy at Athens in connection with the diplomatic complication which resulted on the peace of Nicias. We find that it was first, as was of course necessary, brought before the council, and the next day it was introduced by the Prytanies to the Assembly. In the preliminary hearing before the council there does not appear to have been any discussion of the proposals which the envoys were empowered to make. They simply explained what their powers were. The confusion which resulted arose from their denial in the Assembly that they had full power to treat, after the Prytanies had formally introduced them as plenipotentiaries.

[1] v. 45.

This preliminary meeting was of course necessary merely for formal purposes, as the Prytanies had to summon the Assembly and determine the order of the business; they could not do so till they had had an interview with the ambassadors and learnt what they had come about. This is illustrated by the scene in the Acharnians where the ambassadors from Persia are introduced by the Prytanies. But in this as in the other cases of Probouleuma the peculiar constitution of the council averted the danger of the matter being practically settled before it came to the Assembly. Had all the leading statesmen and orators been members of the council this would surely have been the case.

Character of the council. I think then that I have said enough to show that the βουλή was almost entirely a business body. Its duty was not to discuss questions of policy, nor to decide on momentous matters; it had to dispose of the enormous mass of detailed business which was necessarily connected with the government of the state. Its meetings were not like those of the House of Commons; they would be more like the meeting of a municipal council, a school board, or a committee of a County Council. There would be a great deal of business to be got through, there would probably as a rule be very few members present[1], the matters to be settled would each severally be of very small importance, there would be a good deal of opening for personal favour but very little for political influence. A βουλευτής might

---

[1] Cf. Dem. in Androtionem, 604, 36, where he speaks of a βουλευτής as "hardly ever entering the council chamber."

help a friend or injure an enemy[1]. He could not direct the policy of the city. What was important was that the council should as a rule be without bias, that it should not represent any party or interest, that it should get through its work quickly, and that there should be as little bribery as possible.

There was obviously then no reason at all why *Relation of orators to the council.* orators or statesmen should be members of it; they would be able to give their opinions on any question which directly interested them, their influence would be as great in the council as in the Assembly or in the law-courts, but it would be great not because they had a vote, but because they had the power of persuading other people. Now this removes one of our great difficulties. So long as we speak vaguely of the βουλή as responsible for the safety of the state, and as director of the finances, it is difficult to see how it was possible to exclude the leading men in the state. When we see exactly in what the duties consisted the answer is clear.

Two points to be noticed result from this. The first is the publicity of the meetings.

The meetings of a deliberative assembly may be *Publicity of meet-* public and yet the result be little influenced by the *ings of the council.* opinions of people outside, at any rate by those of individuals. But the meetings of a business body are public in a very different sense; for it must be constantly in communication with people who are not

---

[1] The case given in Aesch. in Timarchum, 109 etc. (127, 28) is an instance where a βουλευτής used his position to help a ταμίας in peculation; how he was enabled to do so we are not informed.

members. There can seldom have been any business brought before the council which did not require the presence of someone who was a stranger, who would have to be interrogated, to give information, or to explain his wishes. Whether it was an official who wanted money for some public purpose, or the representatives of a town which claimed an alleviation of tribute, or Persian ambassadors who had to be introduced to the Assembly, or a trierarch who had lost his ship, or the farmer of a tax, or some man who had discovered an oligarchic conspiracy, or an orator who wished to propose a motion in the Assembly,—all would have to come in person before the council to explain their plan and justify their request[1]. And moreover the council would always be able to summon to their assistance anyone whose special knowledge would be of use. This they would especially do when they wanted the help of skilled advice, and we have frequent references to orators and others who were present in the council without being members of it.

But not only was the council in this way constantly brought into communication with men of all classes in the state, but its sittings were themselves public. This was necessary. The powers of the council were of such a kind as could not be safely entrusted to a body sitting privately. That would have been as dangerous to personal

---

[1] This is shown by the fact recorded in the work already quoted, where the author says that many people had to wait a whole year before they could get the council to attend to their business. [Xenophon] Ἀθηναίων Πολιτεία, iii. 1, etc.

liberty as are law-courts where the hearing is not public.

Had the council been a small body which sat privately, it would have had an almost unlimited power over the whole state. As it was, it sat in public; the citizens could stand round and listen to the proceedings. These proceedings would often be really judicial, sometimes judicial in form. The great numbers of the council would, in important cases, give to its meetings the appearance of one of the jury courts. A case would be brought up for decision: an appeal, for instance, from the assessment of the τάκται, or the confirmation of the appointment of an official. The different parties would plead, they would have speeches written for them by orators; the councillors would sit and listen. There would be a difference from a jury court, because the council would consult together, but the work which they had to do would be of the same kind.

It will appear then that there would be constant opportunities for any orator, who wished to do so, to bring any proposal which fell within its province before the council, to address it himself, to use his eloquence and his influence in the task of persuading the members, and to report to them his view of any matter. He would be able to guide their decisions. We have, in fact, in our records continual reference to the presence of men and orators before the council at a time when they were not members of it[1]. The council often sat as a court of justice, and

---

[1] Lysias XIII. 21, XXII. Andoc. de myst. 154; de reditu, 21.†

then an orator could accuse an enemy before it as
before any other court; when, on the other hand, it
sat as an administrative body, it would be subject to
just the same kind of terrorism which a popular
orator could bring to bear on any other magistrates;
he would bully them[1], and make them do what he
wanted, without being a member, just as much as he
would any other board.

Moreover, the other magistrates, though not
members of the council, were in constant communication with it. This was especially the case with
the generals. All communications to the Assembly
had to be made first to the Prytanies, and the
Prytanies would constantly apply to the generals
and other magistrates for advice and information;
so that in this way the council chamber was the
centre of all public life, it was the connecting link
between all branches of the public service. Not only
was nearly every citizen in turn a member of it,
but each year all the public officials and innumerable other citizens were brought by business affairs
into close connection with it.

*Exception-
al offices.*   If however we would properly understand how it
was that the Athenians could afford to dispense
with "ability" in the council, there is another set
of institutions which we must take into account;
the exceptional offices. These opened to any able or
pushing men an opportunity for action. A man who
was without military ability and had not been chosen

---

[1] Ar. Equites, 166 βουλὴν πατήσεις καὶ στρατηγοὺς κλαστάσεις.
Here the προστάτης τοῦ δήμου is spoken of as being without any
connection with either council or generals.

for any civil duty by the lot, was not thereby deprived of all means of showing his usefulness in office. Suppose he had special knowledge of some public matters—that he took a strong interest in finance, or foreign politics, or the navy, or the improvement of the city. He could not use the regular offices as the sphere of his endeavours, but he could do better; he could have an office created for him. Again, if any branch of the state was in difficulties, or if particular attention was required for the proper working of some department, it was always possible to appoint a special commission to take the matter in hand, and to place on it those citizens who had most knowledge and ability. So, when the financial difficulties became pressing, ζητηταί or πορισταί were appointed to devise new sources of income; foreign affairs were entrusted to ambassadors; were there temples to be built or fortifications to be repaired, a special board of ἐπιστάται or τειχοποιοί was appointed. When Demosthenes was at the height of his power he had no regular office, but was one of a commission of τειχοποιοί, because the defence of the state was a matter with which he was peculiarly concerned. In B.C. 346 Æschines was made special ambassador to the Peloponnesian states in order to try and negociate an alliance against Philip. The building of the Parthenon and Erechtheion, the rebuilding of the long walls in B.C. 395 were entrusted to commissions of this kind. The συγγραφεῖς, who were appointed to superintend the drawing up of a new code of laws, the συνήγοροι, who represented the state in public trials, the ἀποστολεῖς who superintended the fitting out of an expedition,—all these are instances of such exceptional offices[1].

And these were an essential part of the system; they supplied just what was wanted in the council and the ordinary boards; they enabled the Assembly to appoint men of special ability whenever it seemed desirable; but, just because they were exceptional, they did not, as a rule, open the same dangers to the supremacy of the Assembly as would have resulted from regularly elected magistrates. At times indeed they did get so much power as to be a danger to the constitution. The most striking instance of this is the appointment of the $\pi\rho\acute{o}\beta ov\lambda o\iota$ in B.C. 413, with the special duty of advising the state as regards its whole policy; the circumstances made it desirable to have, what hitherto had been wanting, a council which had wisdom. The Thirty again were originally appointed as a small and exceptional commission in order to revise the laws.

In cases such as these the appointment of an exceptional commission changed the whole working of the constitution. Generally it was otherwise; these exceptional offices were simply a means of making the constitution rather more elastic.

A seat in the council was of In this way it was that the council was able to do its work, although it was filled by the lot, and

---

[1] For these cf. infra, p. 103 etc. A good instance of the opening they gave to a determined person is contained in Demosthenes' speech against Androtion, 48. We are told how Androtion got himself appointed as an extraordinary officer to do work generally done by $\kappa\lambda\eta\rho\omega\tau a\grave{\iota}$ $\check{a}\rho\chi a\acute{\iota}$. Cf. also 69, where we find that he was appointed on a special commission to look after the treasures of the Parthenon.

although it had not the advantage of the regular *little use*
presence among its members of the leading men in *to a*
statesman.
the city. Indeed it will be evident that, after all,
a seat in the council would be not only not indis-
pensable to a statesman, but scarcely even desirable.
A member of the council would indeed have great
power; but it would be power like that exercised by
a vestryman. He would be able to influence for
good or bad the lives of many individuals; he could
help a friend, or revenge himself on an enemy; he
could even use his position to procure advantages
for other cities, or to oppress them unjustly. He
could perpetrate innumerable jobs. Power of this
kind is always pleasant and desirable, and it was
the advantage of the democratic constitution that
it gave a share in it to all the citizens; but after all
it was not essential to a great career; a politician
who had made his name and won his reputation
could scarcely add to his influence by a seat in
the council. And the work must have been very
laborious. The position must have been chiefly
grateful to small people; to men who enjoyed the
importance, the bustle, the dignity which attended
the Prytanies. To men of wide ambition and high
position it must have been burdensome.

The peculiar kind of duties performed by the *Dangerous*
council will also give a very good reason for the *powers*
entrusted
particular method of appointment. The council had *to the*
council.
a very wide power over the lives and fortunes of the
citizens; it could interfere in their private life, it
could act at times almost like an inquisition, it had
every opportunity for exercising the greatest op-

pression over individuals. There is no doubt that at
times it did act oppressively and unjustly. It could
easily have become most dangerous to the public
liberty; constituted as it was, the council was still in
times of panic and distress the instrument by which
the power of the state became the instrument of
oppression. The accounts we have of the events
which followed the mutilation of the Hermae show
how real this danger was. It becomes still plainer
when we are told that in times of depression it was
the duty of the council to restore the finances by
discovering people who were in debt to the state[1].
What a possibility of wrong does this open!

That the injustice seldom reached any serious
degree is probably due to the method of appointment; so long as the office was held for a year, so
long as responsibility was strictly enforced, and so
long as all classes were fairly represented in it, the
results would not be very serious. Had the council
been appointed otherwise than by lot the danger
would have been much greater. As it was, the
council was a μικρόπολις; it represented no class;
therefore systematic oppression of one class by another, which is the most dangerous form of injustice,
could not be very serious[2]. Also the lot prevented
organised oppression; so long as no efforts could

---

[1] Demosthenes, Androtion, 607, 47 etc. Ar. Equites, 474,
774—5. Ach. 379,

εἰσελκύσας γάρ μ' εἰς τὸ βουλευτήριον
διέβαλλε καὶ ψευδῆ κατεγλώττισέ μου.†

[2] There was of course always a tendency to act harshly towards
rich people; but this was not stronger in the council than in the

ensure election, the members would not have the community of feeling necessary to successful wrong-doing. Lastly, it was of great importance that the members of the council were in no way members of an official class; a private man was not hampered in his relation to them by his own ignorance of public procedure, or their acquaintance with official forms; this knowledge was spread over the whole city, because every one was at some time an official, and so the worst kind of legal cruelty, which results when the forms of law are used to give to oppression the appearance of justice, was prevented. Injustice there was of course; but it was usually unorganised; a few criminals were left unexecuted, a few innocent men were punished, a few paid too heavy taxes, a few made a little money out of their public duties; but systematic oppression and organised fraud were impossible.

Assembly. All I wish to show is that the council had no opinion or motive of its own, different from that of the citizens as a body, which would make it an instrument of official oppression.

ADDITIONAL NOTE TO CHAPTER II.

On the date of the Introduction of the Lot[1].

It is remarkable that we have no information in any classical author as to the date and occasion of the introduction of the lot. The matter has in consequence become the subject of a controversy[2]. Herodotus in his account of the battle of Marathon refers to Callimachus, who was Polemarch, as "selected by lot" to that office[3]; and Plutarch quotes a statement of Demetrius of Phaleron that Aristeides when he was archon, just after the Persian wars, was "selected by lot from the families who had the greatest possessions[4]." It used therefore to be generally held that the use of the lot was older than the Persian wars. And the general opinion of the ancients that the lot was a democratic institution seemed to imply that it was introduced by someone who wished to develope the democracy. Thus, as the reforms of Cleisthenes are recognised as the most important epoch in the growth of the democracy, it was the obvious conclusion to attribute the introduction of the lot to him, or at least to regard it as a result of the movement which he began.

---

[1] [In the Appendix will be found a discussion of the additional information supplied by the discovery of the Πολιτεία τῶν Ἀθηναίων of Aristotle.]

[2] A full history of the controversy is given by Lugebil in the Jahrbuch für Classische Philologie, Suppl. Bd. v.

[3] Her. vi. 109.

[4] Plut. Arist. i. κυάμῳ λαχὼν ἐκ τῶν γενῶν τῶν τὰ μέγιστα τιμή-ματα κεκτημένων.

Grote and other historians have, however, pointed *Grote's* out that this theory is not without difficulties. For it *view.* is argued first, that if the archons were appointed by lot at a time when only the richer citizens were eligible, the people would lose the power even of electing their rulers; and thus the introduction of the lot, far from being a democratic measure, would be one of the strongest defences of the aristocracy[1]. We must therefore believe that the lot was not applied to the appointment of the archons till the office had been thrown open to all by Aristeides. Further, it is argued in support of this view that the history of the Persian wars is not consistent with the belief that the chief magistrates were appointed by lot. For the two leading men in the state, Themistocles and Aristeides, were both archons just at the time of a great crisis; this, it is urged, cannot have been the result of chance; they must have been elected[2]. The statement of Herodotus about Callimachus must be then simply a mistake; he has applied to a previous generation a custom which prevailed when he was writing. As to Aristeides the tradition as a matter of fact was doubtful even in ancient times. For Plutarch quotes also a passage from Idomeneus to the effect that Aristeides was not chosen by lot, but by popular election[3]. The lot then was introduced sometime after the year 477, and it was

[1] It is a parody of this argument when Müller-Strübing maintains that the lot was therefore introduced as a means of tempering the democracy.

[2] Lugebil adds Xanthippus, the father of Pericles, and Callimachus. The latter we are asked to believe was elected because of his fortunate name. I show below that the "coincidence" does not really exist.

[3] Plut. Arist. i. καὶ μὴν ἄρξαι γε τὸν Ἀριστείδην ὁ Ἰδομενεὺς οὐ κυαμευτόν, ἀλλ' ἑλομένων Ἀθηναίων φησίν.

one of the steps by which the democratic party did
away with the power of the archonship and the
Areopagus, and were able to develope the influence
of the popular jury courts.

† *Difficulties in this.* In a matter of this kind it seems however as though
we ought not to refuse to accept the distinct assertion
of our two best authorities without very strong reasons.
The evidence of Idomeneus is of no weight in the matter,
because Plutarch certainly understood him to mean
that a special exception was made in favour of Aristeides; the evidence of the popular enthusiasm was that
the ordinary rule of election by lot was set aside in his
case. Of the other considerations on which Grote and
those who follow him rely, the first will, I think, lose
its force, if we remember that, when the Greek authors
speak of the lot as democratic, they are always referring
to the system as it existed at Athens after about 450 B.C.
They were acquainted with the lot as an essential part
of the complete democratic constitution, and this is
what is in their minds. The use of the lot was so much
more conspicuous at Athens than elsewhere, that, when
men talked of the lot, they meant the lot as used at
Athens. But they never assert that the lot could not
exist in some form in a state which is not democratic;
in fact we are especially told that it was found in some
aristocracies [1]. What made the lot at Athens democratic was that all citizens were eligible, and that the
number of offices to be filled was very large. It is

---

[1] Cf. Schömann, Alt. p. 154. "In manchen Staaten aber und
zwar wie ausdrücklich bezeugt wird (Anax. Rhetor. ad Alex. c. 2, p.
14), auch in Oligarchien wurde statt der Wahl das Loos angewandt.
Ja, es ist nicht unwahrscheinlich, dass gerade in den älteren
Zeiten diese Besetzungsart am meisten beliebt gewesen sei, und
zwar eben in den Oligarchien.†

absurd to discuss a political institution apart from its
surroundings as if it were an abstract expression. Nor
is there anything in the fact that what I may call the
extended use of the lot was one of the foundations of
the democracy, to prevent us believing that the lot itself
existed at an earlier period in the old aristocracy. (2)
And the other argument is equally unconvincing, for the
simple reason that we know so little about the matter.
Of course if the archon had been really at that time
chosen by lot from all the pentacosiomedimnoi and not
from a few candidates, it would have been remarkable
that Themistocles was successful; but we have no
reason to suppose that this was the case [1].

There is then every reason to believe that the lot *Was the*
was part of the formalities by which the archons were *lot older than Clei-*
chosen before the Persian wars. Have we any reason *sthenes?*
for fixing the introduction of it as late as the time of
Cleisthenes? The chief reason for doing so is the recognition of the fact that the lot was democratic; but if
we remember that what was democratic was not the
selection of nine men among the aristocracy to hold the
archonships, but the selection of hundreds—almost thousands of men from all classes, to fill the council and also
other offices, this argument will fail to convince us that
the lot could not have been used before. And there are
reasons of some strength for believing that it was used.
It was the merit of Fustel de Coulanges[2] to be the first
to point out that, as the lot was religious in its origin,
it must have been in some form or other a custom of
very great antiquity. Also he appealed to some rather

---

[1] Cf. infra, pp. 83—4.

[2] La Cité antique, p. 213. Nouvelle Revue Historique de Droit,
ii. 1878. Cf. for a criticism of this view Revue de Philologie, 1880,
pp. 52 etc.

vague language of Plutarch [1] and Pausanias [2] as proof
that the Greeks knew that the archons had from the
earliest times been chosen by lot. His view has not
met with favour; and it is in our present state of
knowledge difficult to see how it can be reconciled with
the statements of the fact that Solon gave to the people
the power of choosing their rulers [3]. Apart from this it
seems as though his explanation were that which gives
the most satisfactory solution of the difficulty. We
know that in Greece where there was hereditary king-
ship, as at Sparta, the order of succession was not
accurately predetermined; disputed successions often occurred, and to settle them the advice of the gods was
generally taken [4]. We are certainly justified in assuming
that if ever there were hereditary rulers at Athens,
similar disputes took place, and that both sides appealed
to oracles, omens, or the lot for a decision. The rulers
were afterwards taken from a limited number of families instead of from one, they became a college of nine,
and they held office for a limited period; but we cannot imagine that at first the procedure at elections
was clearly determined. Disputed elections would often
occur, and the lot would be naturally appealed to as one
among other ways by which the dispute could be settled [5].

Moreover the analogy of other states makes it probable that the archons had themselves the right if not of
appointing, at least of nominating their successors; and,

[1] Plut. Pericles, 9.

[2] Pausanias, iv. 5; cf. also Dem. in Lept. 90.

[3] Ar. polit. ii. 12, 1274ᵃ 15.

[4] This is worked out by Lugebil, l. c.

[5] I have stated the argument in my own words; it differs
to some extent from the way in which Fustel de Coulanges
expresses it.

in later times, as we know, it was the Thesmothetae
who drew the lots among the candidates. And though
we have no express information it is easy to see how some
combination of nomination and the lot could grow up,
if the magistrates who had the right of nomination were
also the men who in case of a dispute would have to
refer the matter to the gods; whether it was that the
lot was drawn among the candidates nominated by the
different Thesmothetae, or whether the Thesmothetae
decided whom they should nominate by drawing lots
among possible candidates. For, however it was arranged, the candidates must have been limited in
number.

Let us take any period, say in the 7th century,
when there were undoubtedly nine annual archons, who
were chosen from among the Eupatrids alone. I do not
know that we have any means of telling how large this
class was, but all our records point to the fact that they
were only a small portion of the population existing at
that time. But if it be remembered that the number of
male citizens of full age in Athens at the time of
Pericles was according to one account only 14,000, and
certainly not more than 30,000, I think I may safely
assume that in early times the number of male Eupatrids above the age of 17 was considerably less than 1000,
not probably more than 200 or 300. But if this was
the case, and if from these the nine archons had every
year to be elected, it will result that, unless re-election
was common, nearly every Eupatrid would in his turn
be archon. The members of great families would each
one after another as he came of full age hold office for
a year. To each in rotation would come his year for the
archonship; and in a small body such as I am imagin-
ing the rules which determined at what age, or under

6—2

what circumstances it was proper for each to have his
archonship would be carefully handed down by tradition,
and strictly enforced by the spirit of the order. Those
who were in touch with the feeling of the leading men
would know quite well who was marked out each year as
the next person on the roll. Therefore we may imagine
that each year the number of candidates would be very
little, if at all greater than the number of offices to be
filled; and a candidate who was passed over one year
would only have to wait till the next, when he would be
able to come forward with a double claim to be elected.
And we can well understand how the decision might in
such cases be best left to the lot; the question to be
decided was not one of *ability* nor *party*, but simply
of *precedence*; of two candidates the doubt was not
which ought to be archon and which not, but which
ought to be archon this year and which next year, and,
perhaps, which of the different archonships should be
held by each candidate. Thus it would be that a custom
which had originated as a rude way of settling the
claims of rival competitors for kingly power, would
continue as a convenient method of settling the order
in which the nobles should hold the one great office in
the state. When the qualification for election was
made one of property and not of birth, the custom
would still be useful, for so long as property was
measured in land there would be few of the first class
who were not of Eupatrid family, while the practical
supremacy of the nobles would doubtless render it
almost impossible for such an interloper to be a
candidate.

This is no more than an hypothesis; I cannot offer
any proof of it; but it is interesting to make an hypothesis, which at least does not oblige us to contradict

our best authorities. If we adopt it, the difficulties about Themistocles and Aristeides are not so great as they appear. Both were members of Eupatrid families; both would, as a matter of course, succeed in proper course to the archonship; and that Themistocles was archon in one year between the battles of Marathon and Salamis is no great coincidence; had he been archon in 492, or 491, or in any year to 477, it would have been possible to comment upon the remarkable fact that the most able man in the state was chosen just in this year—with no less plausibility than we can now. In whatever year Themistocles had been archon he would doubtless have made his tenure of office remarkable. At any rate, knowing as little as we do of the institutions we are discussing, it hardly seems as though we were justified in using an *a priori* argument to put aside the express statement of Herodotus.

The conclusion I come to then is, that in some form or other the lot had always been used in the selection of the archons, though the method of application doubtless varied. When Aristeides had thrown open the archonship to all citizens and either he, Cleisthenes, or Pericles, had done away with the restrictions upon nominations, the result was that, though the archons were still κναμευτοί, the process had nevertheless completely changed its character. The institution on which the power of the nobles depended was broken down.

It is always more probable that a use like the lot was the growth or relic of some old custom than that it was suddenly introduced. But this applies only to the archonship. The historical difference between it and the other offices is enormous. It was old. They were new. Men were chosen to be archons by lot, because that had always been the custom; for the council[1], for the Apodectai, for the Logistai, for all the other offices, the lot must have been deliberately introduced for political purposes. Whether this was done when these offices were themselves created we do not know; we do not even know when they were created; though it cannot well have been before Cleisthenes, nor after 450 B.C.[2] It is in its application to all these offices that the essentially democratic nature of the lot consists, much more even than in its later use for the archonship. It is a neglect of this truth which has made Fustel de Coulanges overestimate the continued importance of the religious associations[3]; and a similar omission to recognise the essential differences between the two has made Grote and others, who have rightly estimated the political use in later times, ignore the truth that it could have had a quite different value when applied only to the archonship. The discussion on the whole matter is instructive because it shows how easy it is to go wrong by "abstraction," and to look on a custom like "election by lot" as though it had an absolute value,

[1] Fustel de Coulanges suggests that the Prytanies were elected by lot because their duties were originally religious (p. 390). This is very improbable.

[2] The earliest mention of the lot for the council is in an inscription of about 450, which, though it applies to Erythrae, is evidence for the use of the lot at Athens then.†

It is still possible that the discovery of some early inscription will give us certain knowledge on the matter.

[3] After showing rightly enough that the lot was originally religious and must have existed before the democracy, he goes on to say that it never was democratic. "Il n'était pas d'ailleurs un prócédé démocratique," l. c., n. 1. Even if, as he and Curtius suggest, the institution of the generals by Cleisthenes was a democratic measure, that does not in the least affect the point that the lot as afterwards used was still more democratic.

which would be the same at all times and in all circumstances [1].

[1] It does not seem possible to discover with any certainty when election by lot was abandoned.

Bergk, N. Rhein. Museum, xix. 605, refers to an inscription published in the Ephemeris Archæologica, 3793, which contains a list of archons. This is of the time of Mithradates, and in it one man Μήδειος is mentioned as holding the office three years running. This shows that by this time the constitution had been modified, and the archonship was now filled by election from among the richer citizens. The change is generally supposed to have taken place in 146. (Cf. Hertzfeld 'Griechenland unter den Römern,' 310. C. I. A. iii. 87.) For a minor office we find it existing after this. (Cf. C. I. A. iii. 81. Wachsmuth, die Stadt Athen, i. 651.)

I should however expect to find that the alteration was made before this. Whatever the forms may have been, it is impossible that the reality of the democratic constitution can have been maintained so long as this. It is disappointing that nothing is said about the matter in the accounts of the change of constitution in 322 B.C. Cf. Droysen, Hellenismus, II. i. 80—81; Diod. xviii. 18.

CHAPTER III.

THE OFFICIALS.

WE must now turn from the council to a consideration of the other offices to which men were appointed by lot; and in regard to these also, if we would understand the lot, we must consider it in connection with the other parts of the constitution to which it belonged. The lot might be used in other states with other results: at Athens, of which we alone have knowledge, it was only one (though an essential) part of the democratic system. It helped to secure perfect equality among all citizens, a regular rotation in office, and the undisputed authority of the assembly.

Rotation in Office. The system is really the extension of an oligarchic principle to the whole body of citizens. In a strictly oligarchic state the council is supreme, not the assembly; but the council is chosen only from the members of certain families, and all magisterial appointments and all administrative posts of influence are reserved for members of the oligarchic clique. But in such a state, though a seat in the council is for life, the tenure of all other offices is short, and every member of the ruling order has a right to succeed to office in his turn. By this means

the supremacy of the council over all offices is secured as well as equality among those who are
eligible. The lot might have been used to secure
this end, just as it was used at Athens; probably
indeed it was in operation in some states. However
this may be, the principle of rotation in office was not
peculiar to Athens, nor was it essentially democratic.
Aristotle especially recommends it for his πολιτεία,
and he makes it an objection to the state proposed
in the Republic of Plato that there the same men
will always hold office. He maintains repeatedly that
within the select circle of the governing class in any
state it is undesirable to make distinctions, and that
all " peers " ought to have a share in office[1]. What
was done at Athens was to apply the principle which
is found in every oligarchy to a much larger class.
There were to be no half-citizens; a man if he
was a citizen at all was to have his share in the
pleasures and responsibilities of magisterial authority. Here, as in an oligarchy, the Senate consisted
of past or future magistrates : but the past and
future magistrates included all the citizens. The
garland of office came to an Athenian by right of
birth, just as did the fasces to a Metellus, or his
uniform to a Hohenzollern[2].

---

[1] Ar. polit. ii. 2, 1261. Aristotle maintains that, where it is
impossible for the best men always to remain in office, whether
office be good or bad, it is right that all should take part in it.

Cf. ii. 5, 1264[b]. And again viii. 8, 1308[a] he specially recommends
that in a πολιτεία the offices should all be made of short duration,
so that all qualified persons may be admitted.

Cf. also vii. 2, 1317[b].

[2] At Rome the principle was practically maintained that all

Character-istics of Oligarchy and Demo-cracy.

There are however important differences between the working of the principle of rotation in an Oligarchy and a Democracy, since in an oligarchy the officers are few in number, and their duties are in consequence complicated. Accumulation of offices is common; and re-election is practised, if the offices are not held for some considerable period. This is necessary, since the men from whom officials are chosen are few in number. Further, though public responsibility is recognised, and an account can be demanded of the conduct of each official, yet this is generally of but little avail. Account is to be rendered to the same body from whom the magistrates are chosen; the individual is protected by the order to which he belongs, because the interests of all are identical. Each member of the order feels an attack on one of his fellows as a possible curtailment of his own privileges, and the supremacy of the order is endangered when the right of popular criticism is allowed.

At Athens the offices were numerous; all offices were collegiate, and the colleagues were seldom less than ten in number; re-election was almost unknown[1]; accumulation of office rare; office was

members of the senatorial families should succeed in turn to the great offices. Had Rome been governed by a pure oligarchy this could have been done by the lot; as it was, this result was practically secured notwithstanding the nominal existence of popular election.

[1] As we have seen, re-election to the βουλή was possible if not common. For other offices however the matter was different. So far as I am aware, there is no definite statement on the matter in any contemporary authority: but

almost without exception annual[1]. By this means office was opened to the greatest possible number of men: and as a result the work of the office could be greatly simplified, and the duties strictly defined by law. As a result of this, one of the characteristics of the Democracy was a careful organisation and a consequent high standard of administrative efficiency, and this was accompanied by a greater freedom from fraud or dishonesty than was possible in an oli-

(A) It is impossible to find a single case occurring of re-election to any office which was filled by the lot. We know the names of a large number of officials, especially ταμίαι, ἐλληνοταμίαι and ἐπιμεληταί, and among them we never find one man twice holding the same office.

(B) In one of the προοιμία δημηγορικά, printed in Demosthenes' works, we find the statement παντάπασι τὸν αὐτὸν τρόπον, ὦ ἄνδρες Ἀθηναῖοι, ὅνπερ τοὺς ἱερεῖς, οὕτω καθίστατε καὶ τοὺς ἄρχοντας. δεινό-τατοι γάρ ἐστ' ἀφελέσθαι μὲν ὅσ' ὑμῖν ὑπάρχει, καὶ νόμους περὶ τούτων θεῖναι, ἄν τις ἀστυνομήσῃ δὶς ἢ τὰ τοιαῦτα, στρατηγεῖν δ' ἀεὶ τοὺς αὐτοὺς ἐᾶν. Also in one of the documents inserted in the speeches of Demosthenes we find a similar statement:—οὐδὲ δὶς τὴν αὐτὴν ἀρχὴν τὸν αὐτὸν ἄνδρα (καταστήσω), a clause in the oath of the Heliasts. Dem. in Timocratem, 150.

These passages though of late origin were probably written by men who could easily find out the truth on this point, and, as they are supported by evidence from our lists, we are justified by them in stating that re-election was absolutely forbidden.

Aristotle polit. vii. 2, 1317[b], tells us that in a democracy re-election will not be allowed : τὸ μὴ δὶς τὸν αὐτὸν ἄρχειν μηδεμίαν ἢ ὀλιγάκις ἢ ὀλίγας ἔξω τῶν κατὰ πόλεμον.

[1] Aristotle specially recommends that office be not held for any long period:—

polit. vii. 2, 1317[b] τὸ ὀλιγοχρονίους τὰς ἀρχὰς ἢ πάσας ἢ ὅσας ἐνδέχεται, and viii. 8, 1308[a] οὐ γὰρ ὁμοίως ῥᾴδιον κακουργῆσαι ὀλίγον χρόνον ἄρχοντας καὶ πολύν.

Revolutions, he adds, come from long tenure of office.

garchy[1]; and the publicity which was secured to all
public action enabled the state to enforce in the
most stringent manner an enquiry into the whole
conduct of its magistrates: each official had to
submit to a general criticism of his conduct, and in
particular to a detailed examination of all his expenditure.

In some states a magistrate has power direct
and underived; in others he gains influence as the
member of a ruling class whose interest it is to
protect and support each individual. In Athens the
magistrate was unprotected; he was surrounded by
no veil of mystery; he was simply the man chosen
from the people to do certain things. Whilst his
commission lasted he was backed by all the authority
which he derived from the people; the moment it
was over he became again an ordinary citizen, with
nothing to protect him but his integrity or ability.
The Athenians are the only people where the magistrates always remained the servants of the state.

*Con-
venience
of the Lot.* It will I think be evident how natural and
convenient an arrangement the lot was, as a means
of attaining these ends. Let us try to imagine
the Athenian democracy without the lot. Here is
a state of between 20,000 and 30,000 citizens; there
are hundreds of offices to be filled every year. These
offices are all annual; no two may be held at the
same time, and to most of them re-election is forbidden. If we remember too that the richer citizens
were constantly occupied with onerous public services,
and that the poorer were constantly required to serve

[1] On the morality of public officials at Athens cf. infra, p. 174.

in the army, we shall find that the scope for choice among those willing to serve cannot have been very large. If the system was to be kept up, the services of every one would be wanted; it would have been absurd and futile to try and pick out men for their ability or character. For the question which had always to be decided was not "Shall this man be a magistrate, or not?" but "Shall he be a magistrate this year, or next," or "Shall he have this office, or some other?" and as this was a matter of extremely little importance, it showed good practical common sense on the part of the Athenians that they answered it in the easiest and most direct manner by casting lots.

There is one important difference between the council and the other offices. In the council men of *Different classes of magistrates.* all ranks and classes sat together; in the other offices a certain distinction of rank was maintained. Some offices, as the archonship, entailed a considerable expenditure, and moreover the preliminary examination was very strict; we may therefore reasonably believe that the candidates for it were drawn almost entirely from the well-to-do old-established families. For some offices, as that of treasurer to the goddess and Hellenotamias, no one could be chosen except members of the first class; the duties being of such a kind that they could not be safely entrusted to anyone who had not a considerable property, which would be a pledge to the city for his honesty[1]. The duties to be performed by other officials were both disagreeable and laborious;

[1 See Appendix. This law it appears was not really observed.]

it is probable that they were paid for undertaking them, and we may therefore reasonably suppose that men of birth and position would willingly give up these to others who were glad to get the money and did not find the work repulsive. The eleven, the agoranomoi, the astunomoi, may probably be counted among these inferior offices. Of course in a perfect democracy there would have been no distinctions of this kind; but the Athenians did not allow respect for a word or an idea to lead them beyond what was practicable and prudent.

The use of the lot is then explained as being the simplest method of attaining the desired end, that all citizens should take their turn in office. The people deliberately did not exercise the right of selection. To do so would have been to interfere with the principle of rotation.

Was office compulsory ? It might be objected that the complete establishment of this principle would require that men should be compelled to serve whether they applied or not. Whether this was the case, or not, we cannot tell: our information as to the proceedings is unfortunately so small that we do not know what the method of nomination was. However, though we have no proof of the matter, it would, I imagine, hardly be too rash to assert that the state did reserve to itself the right of compelling men to hold office, and that the retiring magistrates or others who directed the election could, if necessary, nominate without their consent the candidates among whom the lots should be drawn. If this was not commonly done, it was because there was no reluctance to take office, and no deficiency in the number of voluntary candidates. We may still discover that for some of the more arduous and less profitable offices it was the regular procedure. In the absence of all information, it seems just as probable that the inspectors of the dockyards were selected by the lot from among a certain number of men nominated according to some recognised rule by the ἐπιμεληταὶ τῆς φυλῆς, as from candidates who were nominated at their own request.

We do, in fact, once find the office of treasurer to the goddess spoken of as a λῃτουργία[1]; and the principle of compulsory service was so clearly recognised that there would be no scruples about applying it if necessary. Office among the Athenians was a position of such danger that we may be surprised that we do not hear more directly of compulsion. If it was found necessary, it would however be only for the higher offices, which required a large outlay of money and were not paid, and in which also any real or fancied neglect of duty was most severely punished[2]. We have evidence on the other hand that many of the offices were much coveted; chiefly, apparently, because of the gain they brought.

It is necessary, if we would understand the

---

[1] Andocides, de mysteriis, 132, ἀλλὰ τοὐναντίον λῃτουργεῖν οὗτοι προύβάλλοντο, πρῶτον μὲν γυμνασίαρχον Ἡφαιστείοις, ἔπειτα ἀρχιθεωρὸν εἰς Ἰσθμὸν καὶ Ὀλυμπιάζε, εἶτα δὲ ταμίαν ἐν πόλει τῶν ἱερῶν χρημάτων.

[2] Antiphon, de morte Herodis, 69, tells a story of how one year all the Hellenotamiai but one were put to death on a charge of peculation; and how afterwards it was discovered that they were innocent.

Athenian system, to get rid entirely of the natural prejudice we feel against the lot. This prejudice is so strong that we are always inclined to think the Athenians must have shared our distrust of it; and attempts have often been made to show that this was the case. Historians have appealed to two facts to prove this:—to the institution of the δοκιμασία, and to the fact that a large number of officials were appointed by popular election, and not by the lot. I think, however, that a short examination of these two points will help to prove my position, (1) that the Athenians felt no distrust of the lot, but regarded it as the most natural and the simplest way of appointment; (2) that, in consequence, the general rule was that all magistrates were appointed by the lot: the only exceptions (in the first period of the democracy) being those who had military or semi-military duties, and those who held exceptional appointments which were outside the ordinary routine administration of the state.

The Doki-masia. The popular account of the δοκιμασία is that it was an institution invented to check the worst results of the lot[1]: men, we are told, felt so much distrust of its working that they prepared a means of interfering with its action. It was an opportunity given to the people to prevent someone, who had been legally appointed, from holding office, on no other grounds than that they held him unfit to do so. This

[1] Busolt, Gr. Gesch. vol. ii. p. 469. Gegen die schlimmsten Zufälligkeiten des Looses schützte man sich durch die Prüfung oder Dokimasie. Gilbert, St. i. 208—10, takes the same view though less decidedly.†

view is founded on the statements of the orators:
and there is no doubt that, in the 4th century, the
δοκιμασία was used as a means of preventing men
who were suspected of oligarchic sentiments from
holding an office which they had won by the lot or
otherwise[1]. It is, as I have elsewhere pointed out,
from the observation of this fact that a great deal of
the difficulty about the lot has arisen. If however
my view of the lot is correct, it will be necessary
to some extent to restate our account of this phenomenon. It was, I believe, an abuse which had
grown up at the end of the Peloponnesian war, and
was a direct result of the shock given to the whole
state by the two oligarchic revolutions. If we
look below the speeches of the orators to the
constitution of the court, it is obvious that the
δοκιμασία was not introduced simply to rectify the
verdict of the lot: men chosen by popular elections
were just as much subject to it. It was not the
intention to allow the popular voice a veto on any
appointment by means of an accusation of "incivism."
The object of the δοκιμασία was simply to keep out
of office men who were legally incapacitated. Men
who were not complete citizens by birth, who were
not of a certain age, who were in debt to the state
or who had incurred ἀτιμία by committing certain
offences, were by the laws excluded from office;

---

[1] Cf. Lysias, Or. 26. 16 *passim*; esp. 26, § 9, ὁ θεὶς τὸν περὶ
τῶν δοκιμασιῶν νόμον οὐχ ἥκιστα περὶ τῶν ἐν ὀλιγαρχίᾳ ἀρξάντων ἕνεκα
ἔθηκεν. This cannot be true unless the δοκιμασία was a quite new
institution : but if it was we should expect some more special
reference to its introduction.

and some offices could only be held by men possessed of a certain property. Now it was one of the
characteristics of the Athenian constitution that it
provided a definite regular way of doing everything
however unimportant: nothing was left uncertain.
Supposing anyone were chosen by lot or by popular
election whose qualification was doubtful, considerable inconvenience might arise if there were no
regular procedure for dealing with the matter. To
guard against this, the δοκιμασία was introduced.
The proceedings were as a rule almost formal: they
consisted in putting to the newly elected magistrate
certain questions; if they were satisfactorily answered
the matter was at an end: if it appeared that the
man did not possess some of the qualifications he
was excluded. The δοκιμασία answered the same
sort of purpose as when a candidate for a scholarship
at a school or university is required to produce a
certificate of birth. It was the opportunity which
the official had of proving his legal qualifications:
an opportunity which there must be somehow in
every state; and it is chiefly interesting as showing
the great care taken by the builders of the constitution to procure efficiency by providing beforehand
a means of settling all points[1].

[1] The best account of the matter is given by Hermann,
Staatsalterthümer, 149. Schömann's account is also good: he
says, " the δοκιμασία had nothing to do with the knowledge and
ability requisite for the administration of the office, but only
with the question whether the birth of the man fulfilled the
conditions required, and whether his life had been free from
crime. Those offices for which a special capacity was necessary
which could not be expected of every citizen were filled by popular

It was however possible that the candidate was not satisfied with the justice or validity of the verdict of the revising court; this would especially be the case when, as often happened, private or political enemies had by their evidence procured his rejection. In a case of this kind there would be a dispute either of fact or law to be decided[1]: a dispute which might turn on the status of the mother of the candidate, or on the interpretation of some law disqualifying a particular class of persons. This dispute would have to be decided before a law-court, but the question would still be not, "Is it *wise* to let this man be elected?" but, "Is this man legally disqualified?"

The orators of course in these as in all other cases tried to bias the minds of the jury, and where it was convenient to do so did not shrink from boldly stating that the δοκιμασία ought to take the form of an enquiry into the whole career of a citizen to

election, and it was assumed that the people would not choose anyone of whose capacity it was not sufficiently convinced. On the other hand the people willingly had confidence that everyone who decided to become a candidate for any of the other offices which were filled by lot, would have the requisite capacity, and in fact was not so far wrong in this as may appear at first sight." This is one of the cases where it seems to me that the new school of historians have not improved on their predecessors.

[1] So in Lysias, Or. 26, de Evandro. The real case is that Evander has committed certain acts which disqualify for office: the defence is that he is defended by the amnesty (§ 16): the speaker tries to create a prejudice against Evander and to make the case turn on what is best for the city; and so far as he can makes it seem a question of the personal character of himself and his opponents.

see if he were fit to bear office[1]; but this was just as
much an abuse as when in any ordinary civil suit
they introduced extraneous matter in order to influence the minds of the jury. No doubt they often
succeeded. Many men, probably, were excluded from
office on account of their oligarchic opinions, but this
was a development caused by peculiar circumstances.
Owing to the political struggles of the time a considerable number of men had become ἄτιμοι and
disqualified for office: so far as the δοκιμασία
excluded them it was not (except in cases where it
was abused) an original expression of popular feeling,
it was only the method of putting into execution a
principle already established[2]. We might find the
nearest English parallel to it in the laws respecting
the Roman Catholics. When they were disqualified
by their religion from being elected or appointed to
any post, the law was enforced by requiring every
person who was elected or appointed to take the
Sacrament. This was the δοκιμασία. By taking
the Sacrament a man declared that he was not a
Roman Catholic. At the same time it was open
to anyone to give information that the man was
really a secret Romanist, and thereby still get him
excluded. Now no one would say that the ex-

---

[1] e. g. Lysias, pro Mantitheo, 9, δοκεῖ δέ μοι ἐν ταῖς δοκιμασίαις
δίκαιον εἶναι παντὸς τοῦ βίου λόγον διδόναι.

[2] So in Lysias, Or. 26, § 10, the argument seems to be :—a man
who served as knight under the Thirty may not be a βουλευτής,
much more must a man who has done what this man has done
be ineligible for the archonship: the speaker appeals to the law
and says any reasonable interpretation of it will exclude him.

istence of this and similar laws implied distrust of popular elections, or of appointment by government. But it is just what happened at Athens: only at Athens no one was excluded because of his opinions, only because he had committed certain actions.

The inconveniences which may result from any uncertainty as to the legal qualifications of a man who has been appointed to a public office are so great that no further explanation is required why the Athenians should have taken care that the validity of the appointment should be thoroughly tested before the new officer entered upon his duties. Such a test there must always be. The only peculiarity of the Athenian system was that the name of the procedure, and (to a great extent) the procedure itself, was identical for all offices and all appointments. We disguise the similarity under difference of name; we talk of the registration of voters, the confirmation of bishops, election petitions; but these are all only more cumbrous methods of doing what the Athenians did simply and in the same way for all offices by the δοκιμασία.

The fact that the Athenian courts did not always give an impartial verdict, and in fact did not even profess to do so, was a result of the whole constitution of the judicial system; but it need not affect our judgment of the initial advantages of having some such procedure. At any rate the Athenian dicasteria were not more open in their disregard of the legal aspect of a case than was the House of Commons in

the days when it used to hear election petitions[1].

*Elected
Officials.*

If we turn now to the second point, the consideration of those offices which were not filled by lot, we
shall not I think find any reason to suppose that the
Athenians looked on the lot with distrust, or regarded it as anything exceptional.

†   There are always certain things which can only
be done by men of special ability; there must be
cases in which the dangers which arise from possible
incompetence are greater than any which come from
the possibility that the magistrate will gain undue
influence or misuse his power. This even the
Athenians recognised; election by lot was with
them the rule, but they never attempted to make

*Military
posts.*

it a rule without an exception. The exceptions
were however as few as possible. Of the regular
magistrates only those were elected who were
occupied with the actual command of men in war,
or in the half-military establishments connected
with the public education of the citizens. Much
has been said about the στρατηγοί: it has been truly

[1] A curious contrast to the simplicity of the Athenian constitution might be found in the difficulty experienced in England of
getting an authoritative decision on the qualifications for voting
in any representative body. The uncertainty about the right of
women to sit in a county council could not have occurred there,
because the matter would at once have been brought before a
special court which had to decide all such cases: and it would
have been impossible that such a state of things should result
as has been seen in England, when someone continues to exercise
an office to which he has no claim because it is no one's duty
to take steps in order to deprive him of it.

pointed out that at one period their power was very great, and the office to some extent an object of ambition for those who wished to direct the politics of the city; but the board of the στρατηγοί were never other than generals[1]. Their duties were always, primarily, the management of naval and military matters; secondarily, they at times represented the state in its intercourse with other states and had jurisdiction over foreigners residing in the city. Political power they sometimes had: but it was chiefly because they were men who had influence as speakers and statesmen in the assembly. They were men of ability, and their experience was valuable: hence they were consulted by the governing assemblies. They were, as generals, responsible for the safety of the state: hence any request which came from them, or any warning which they might give, was attended to at once. If they represented to the πρυτάνεις that there was business of urgent importance to be discussed, it was matter of tradition if not of law that the assembly should be summoned[2]. They had the right of bringing all matters before the council, and with the council they were often chosen to represent the people in its intercourse with foreign powers; like all Athenian magistrates, even the lowest, they had extensive judicial duties, and they had as a necessary result of

---

[1] This is shown clearly by the references to them in the Memorabilia of Xenophon. Socrates always speaks of the power of commanding an army as the first requisite of a general. Cf. iii. 1, 6; iii. 4:

[2] C. I. A. i. 40, *ad finem.*

their military power a large authority in financial
matters. But it was their military duties which
were the foundation of their power; and it was
because of them that their appointment was never
made by the lot. I do not know anything so
remarkable as the fact that, notwithstanding the
exceptional position which they occupied, these
generals never did win a position independent of
the assembly. It is not the extent but the limit of
their authority which astonishes us.

If we add to the generals the subordinate military
officials, the ἵππαρχος and φύλαρχος and ταξίαρχος,
and certain other men who, like the σωφρονισταί or
ἐπιμεληταὶ τῶν ἐφήβων, superintended the education
of the young men, we shall, with the doubtful exception of a few unimportant religious officials, find
no regular officials who were not appointed by lot[1].

*Excep-
tional
Offices.*
In all other cases where we are told that a man
was elected to an official position we find that the
office itself was an exceptional institution. I have
already to some extent explained the importance of
these offices, and shown how useful they were in
supplementing the more established procedure. The

[1] There are many offices concerning which our information is
defective, e.g. the τριηροποιοί and the ἑλληνοταμίαι. The ἐκλογεῖς
mentioned in C. I. A. i. 38 (cf. Harpocr. *sub voc.* ἡρέθησαν γὰρ
ἐκλογεῖς παρ' ἡμῖν οἷς πλεῖστα ἐδόκει χρήματα εἶναι) were men chosen
to collect arrears of tribute from the allies. They were exceptional
officers and their duties were partly military, as they had command
over one or more triremes. Cf. Boeckh, Staats. d. A. p. 190.
The same is true of the τάκται, who were probably identical with
οἱ ἐπὶ τὰς πόλεις whose election (χειροτονία) is mentioned C. I. A.
i. 37.

most important of them are the numerous appointments for exceptional service as legate to a foreign
power, or as representative of the state at some religious festival. If an embassy had to be sent to treat †
with a foreign king, if the help of Dionysius was
sought against Thebes or the help of Thebes against
Philip, or if it was desired to break up an alliance between Sparta and Persia, or to send a representative
to the Amphiktyonic council, for this purpose men
of ability and knowledge, leaders in the political
world, must be chosen; and so the lot could not
be used. Also those who were elected to these
offices were temporarily surrounded with a pomp
and importance which marked them out from their
fellow citizens. These appointments had a dignity
of their own, they were highly paid, they gave
opportunities for gaining exceptional experience
and knowledge, they gave to those who held them
peculiar advantages of a kind which democracy
sought to make common to all citizens. Hence
we find that such offices were looked on with
suspicion, and that their holders were the object of
envy. They were oligarchical in their nature; not
because they were filled with oligarchs, but because
a state where such offices abounded would be oligarchic[1]. But oligarchic as they were, they were
not in the least party posts. Election to them was
not conducted on party lines. There were private
societies which would support those of their members
who were candidates; but there was no organisation
to support candidates of particular opinions. If

[1] Cf. the first scene in the Acharnians, also *ib.* vv. 595 etc.

an embassy was to be chosen, the people did not take trouble to choose ambassadors committed to one line of policy. They did not attempt to bind themselves to a particular line by electing men pledged to support it. They elected men who took interest in, or had knowledge of the question; but they elected men of the most opposite opinions[1]. We see how in the case of offices to which election was by vote the influence of the lot extended; the same strictness of account, the same complete obedience to the Assembly, the same collegiateness, the same absence of party organisation is found in the one as in the other: but it was only because elected officials were the exception that elections were so quiet, so business-like, and elected officials so obedient.

Commissioners of public works. Another class of men who were certainly in most cases appointed by the people were the "Commissioners of Public Works" (ἐπιστάται τῶν δημοσίων ἔργων) including the special boards appointed to superintend the building of fortifications and triremes[2]. These, however, do not really form an exception to

[1] E.g. Xen. Hell. vi. 3 in the embassy to Sparta we find men of different parties, including those of the anti-Laconian party. So too in the famous embassy to Philip the leaders of the opposing parties both took part.

[2] Aesch. in Ctesiphontem, § 31. Demosthenes was appointed τειχοποιός by his own tribe Pandionis. There is a distinction between κληρωταὶ ἀρχαί and ἐπιστάται τῶν δημοσίων ἔργων: and though Aeschines contends that these latter are ἀρχαί, he certainly implies that they were never κληρωταί (13—14, 28—30). C. I. A. ii. 830 τειχοποιοὶ αἱρεθέντες. Cf. Wachsmuth, Die Stadt Athen, vol. ii. p. 13, n. 1; ib. p. iv—v.

the rule, because, certainly in the greater number of cases of which we have record, these Commissioners are not members of a permanent bureau. The office is created for a special and exceptional purpose, and expires when the building or repairs with which it is concerned is completed. There is one commission for the building of the Propylæa[1]; one for the building of the Erechtheum[2]; another for the restoration of a temple which had been destroyed by fire[3]. A board of τειχοποιοί is appointed to superintend the rebuilding of the walls in 395[4]; another, of which Demosthenes is a member, in 338[5]. These appointments no more belong to the ordinary constant system of the administration than do the posts of ambassador; or the special commissions of enquiry appointed at times of panic; or the συνηγορεῖς appointed to represent the state in public prosecutions. This is shown by other signs. The regular Athenian boards have almost invariably 10 members; the numbers of these commissions vary, we find sometimes two[6], sometimes three[7], at times five[8], or

---

[1] C. I. A. i. 314.   [2] C. I. A. i. 322.

[3] C. I. A. ii. 829.

[4] C. I. A. ii. 830—32. Cf. Wachsmuth, Die Stadt Athen, ii. p. 5, and p. 13, n. 1.†

[5] Aeschines, l. c. We also find a commission of ten men to investigate the gifts given to the temple of Aesculapius (C. I. A. ii. 836), one for the restoration of the temple of Zeus Soter (C. I. A. ii. 834) and for the building of the Skeuotheke (C. I. A. ii. 1054), and one to superintend the making of two statues ἐπιστάται τοῖν Νίκαιν (C. I. A. iv. 331ᵉ and C. I. A. i. 318.)†

[6] C. I. A. ii. 167.   [7] C. I. A. i. 318, 322.

[8] C. I. A. ii. 834; C. I. A. iv. 331ᵉ.

ten[1]. The regular appointments are, nearly invariably, for a year; in some cases at least, these commissioners hold office for longer[2]; and it is probable that the appointment was generally made to continue till the work entrusted to them was finished[3].

It is certain therefore that many of these commissions must be classed among the exceptional offices, and in consequence it is probable that their members were allowed more power and freedom than could have belonged to men appointed by lot, and that the direct responsibility for the plan and method of building rested with them; also, that the people entrusted to them the right of controlling the architect. Thus they would not only propose in the assembly the general plan of the building, but would be empowered to use their own discretion in the arrangement of details.

The actual charge of the work of course belonged to a professional architect; who was appointed sometimes, if not always, by the people[4]. The chief duties of the commissioners were to examine the plan prepared by him, to see that it would answer the purpose of the building required, to draw up a formal document and sign it. They also had to watch over the progress of the work, and, especially, all payments were made by them to the contractors and workmen. The sale of the

---

[1] Aesch. l. c. In C. I. A. ii. 1054 one only is mentioned as signing the contract, but he possibly acts on behalf of his colleagues.

[2] C. I. A. i. 301 (p. 160), 318.

[3] This was not however always the case. C. I. A. i. 303—309.†

[4] C. I. A. ii. 167, v. 6.

contract seems to have belonged not to them but to the Poletai.

The question, however, suggests itself whether, besides these exceptional commissions appointed to conduct large and important building operations, there were not other and more permanent officials entrusted with the care and preservation of the fabric of the buildings and fortifications already made. I am not aware of any record of such officials, and it is more probable that, so far as this duty did not belong to the province of the priests, treasurers and generals, it was included in the general supervision over all public matters which belonged to the council. This seems to be borne out by the fragment of a decree[1], either of the council or assembly, which provides for building some additional wall on the Acropolis. In the portions preserved we find mention of the Poletai, and of a man who is apparently the architect, but none of any commissioners; and the probable explanation is that where only some small piece of work was to be done the matter was left to the discretion of the architect, and it was not held to be necessary to have a special committee appointed to control him. The payments could of course always be made by one of the regular boards of officials, and the contract as usual would be made by the Poletai. The ἐπιστάται were only appointed when a special work of some magnitude was to be taken in hand[2].

---

[1] Bulletin de Corr. Hell. 1890, p. 177. It seems to belong to the middle of the fifth century.†

In another we find that the control over the architect is given to the ἱεροποιοί. C. I. A. iv. 27[b], l. 11.   [2] [See Appendix.]

With these the exceptions end. There were no
other duties which it did not seem to the Athenian
statesman that any of his fellow citizens could
perfectly well fulfil. For the two great departments of finance and justice, there were in the great
days of the Athenian Democracy no elected officers.
What taxes were to be raised; what money was to
be spent; that the demos in its sovereign power
decided. How much money was necessary for one
department; how much could be afforded for another;
that the council reported. But to raise money, and
spend it; to collect taxes, and proceed against
defaulters; to sell confiscated property, and let public
land; to pay the bills, and audit the accounts;—for
all this there were none but κληρωταὶ ἀρχαί.

Therefore we shall be justified in saying that
neither the institution of the δοκιμασία nor the existence of these exceptional offices shows any distrust
of the lot. This was the ordinary system of appointment, and was deliberately maintained as the wisest
means of preserving the democratic constitution. But
if we are prepared to recognise that election by lot
was the rule and not the exception, we have still
to enquire how it was that the state could exist
and prosper with it, and what the results of the
system were. I propose therefore to explain, so
far as is possible, the manner in which the system
worked, so that we may see what the effects of this
peculiar arrangement were. I shall begin by discussing the financial administration.

CHAPTER IV.

FINANCE.

§ 1. *General Direction.*

IN a modern state the most important political event of the year is the budget. The chief duty of the Government is to estimate the expenses of the coming year, and to propose some method of raising sufficient money to meet the expenses. The question has often been asked how it happened that in antiquity, and especially in Athens, matters of finance had not the same importance[1].

The difference is however more in appearance than in fact. It arises to a great extent from the character of the records. Historians occupy themselves much more with the moral than the economic side of history. Writing with a view to artistic effect, they pass over matters of finance which are supposed to be dull. But the speeches of the orators, and the great mass of inscriptions which have been discovered, show conclusively—what we might have guessed—that, even in the fifth century, finance was almost as important a part of public business as it

---

[1] Boeckh, Staatshaushaltung, Bk. ii. § 1.

is now. Athens had no exemption in this matter. She was subject to the ordinary laws which govern the life of states. Then, as now, it was supply which occupied the minds of leaders of the state; for money meant food for the citizens, good pay for the fleet, new triremes, new fortifications. It meant comfort at home, and supremacy abroad. Then, as now, no leader of the state could keep his position without meeting the financial problem; and the administration of Pericles, of Cleon, of Aristophon, and of Eubulus was then, as it would be now, chiefly judged by their financial policy[1].

There is, however, a point in the constitution of Athens, resulting from the peculiar character of the relations between the officials and the assembly, which tends to obscure this fact.

Absence of a supreme finance official. The first question we naturally ask is:—"Who was the responsible financial adviser; whose duty was it to frame plans for providing money?" It is of the very elements of business that there should be some one whose special duty it is to survey the whole income and expenditure. Without this what would all the care and prudence in details avail?

But at Athens there is great difficulty in discovering with whom this responsibility lay. We can trace the course of a sum of money from one department to another. We can find out how payments were made, where money was kept, who paid it, and who spent it; but where was the central control? All taxes were indeed imposed by the

[1] Cf. Lysias, κατὰ 'Επικράτους xxvii. 3, ὁπόταν ἐν χρήμασιν ᾖ καὶ σωθῆναι τὴν πόλιν καὶ μή.

assembly, and all expenses sanctioned by them. But who advised the assembly, and how did it learn exactly what money was wanted? There must surely have been someone who had a special knowledge of the matter, who could put forward an authoritative statement, and with whom the responsibility of mismanagement would rest.

In the latter half of the 4th century there was such an official: the ταμίας τῆς κοινῆς προσόδου, or ὁ ἐπὶ τῇ διοικήσει. And it has been maintained that this office was in existence at least from the times of the Persian wars. Boeckh and others have supposed that it was held by Aristeides and Pericles and Cleon; and that by holding it they gained their official position, and their right to speak with authority and advise the people. There seems however to be no good authority for the existence of this office before the middle of the 4th century, and it was probably introduced by Eubulus about 352[1]. †

[margin note: ταμίας τῆς κοινῆς προσόδου.*]*

It appears indeed, strange as it may seem, that during the 5th century there was no finance minister. There was no one who was officially responsible for

[1] Plutarch, it is true, speaks of Aristeides as ἐπιμελητὴς τῶν κοινῶν προσόδων, and there are expressions in the *Knights* of Aristophanes (v. 948) which have been supposed to imply that Cleon was officially "ταμίας" of the city. Against this is to be put the complete absence of any reference at all to such an office in inscriptions, and any certain reference in contemporary literature. Cf. infra, p. 117, n. 1, the passages quoted from the Memorabilia. Even in the *Knights*, the prize for which Cleon and the sausage-seller contend is represented as the ascendency in the assembly (τῆς Πυκνὸς τὰς ἡνίας, v. 1109), not election to any office.

H. 8

these matters.   There were numerous subordinate
officials ; but they were all appointed by lot, and had
thereby neither claim nor power to direct the policy
of the city.   There was the council, which with its
important duties was the centre and pivot of the
whole system; but it was after all a body of 500
men taken by lot; it could scarcely be that the
Athenians would look to it for wisdom and advice.

Financial   The constitutional advisers of the assembly were
duties of   not the officials, nor the council, nor even necessarily
the
orators.   the generals. They were the orators[1]. It was on their
energy and ambition that the direction of the finances
depended, as did the supreme control of all departments.   And the Athenians could afford to trust to
them for advice, for, so long as political ambition
was keen, and success in public life the great desire
of every able man, the people knew that these
matters would not be neglected.   The competition
was too vigorous.   If a young man wished to distinguish himself, he must do so by winning the ear
of the assembly.   To do this, he must be able to
criticise the plans of others, or formulate plans of
his own ; to show how money could be saved, or how
it could be better spent.   Whether he dealt with
naval matters, the relations to the allies, the adorn-
ment of the city, or the celebration of public festivals ; if he wished to make an effect, and win reputation, he must have command of the question of
supply.   No one could hope to win a permanent

[1] Dem. xiv. (περὶ συμμοριῶν) 2.

place who did not show a thorough acquaintance with the finance of the city[1].

There is an admirable illustration of this in the Memorabilia of Xenophon[2]. Socrates is represented as conversing with Glaucon, a young man who without adequate knowledge and experience is trying to push himself forward. He wishes προστατεύειν τῆς πόλεως, and Socrates shows him how many things he must know if he wishes to do this; he must understand all about the income of the state and the expenditure; he must know the relative strength of Athens and other states; he must know whence the food supply of the city comes. Now Glaucon is not coming forward to stand for any office; he does not aim at being "public treasurer," or "general;" he is much too young to be eligible: but he wishes to become popular with the assembly, and to do what he likes in the city. He, if he becomes προστάτης τοῦ δήμου, will also "administer the affairs of the city." Now what this and other conversations show is that numbers of young

---

[1] We are told of almost every well-known man, that he occupied himself with finance. I have collected a few instances for which I am chiefly indebted to Beloch (Att. Politik).

Cleophon, Lysias xix. 48. Aesch. ii. 76.

Agyrrhius, Schol. ad Ar. Ranæ, 367, Schol. ad Arist. Eccl. 102. τὸν μισθὸν δὲ τῶν ποιητῶν συνέτεμε καὶ πρῶτος ἐκκλησιαστικὸν δέδωκεν.

Archedemus, Xen. Hell. 1. vii. 2. Ἀρχέδημος ὁ τοῦ δήμου τότε προεστηκὼς καὶ τῆς διωβελίας ἐπιμελόμενος. This probably refers to an exceptional office created at the time. Cf. supra p. 72; cf. Boeckh, St. p. 282.

Callistratus, Theop. Fr. 95. Καλλίστρατος ὁ Καλλικράτους δημαγωγὸς...τῶν δὲ πολιτικῶν πραγμάτων ἦν ἐπιμελής.

[2] Xen. Mem. iii. 6.

men would try to enter on a political career without requisite knowledge, but that anyone who wished to succeed would be obliged, at least to some extent, to acquire it. The system did not ensure that the best advice would be taken, nor the wisest man successful, but it did ensure that there would be plenty of people doing as much as they could to learn about finance, and other matters.

And though there was no official responsible to the assembly, every Athenian would always know whose duty it was to give advice in financial and other matters. He did not feel the want of a public treasurer. If he wished to know the state of public affairs, he listened to the προστάτης τοῦ δήμου: for anyone who had become προστάτης could only keep his position by constantly being able to give on every point what seemed to be the wisest counsel. Thus, when Pericles advised the people to go to war with Sparta, he had to make to them a full statement of all the resources of the state, and showed how by following his advice they had acquired a treasure equal to any demands likely to be made on it. Again, when Cleon was leader of the people, he used and strengthened his power by his financial innovations: it is this which makes his policy, and gives character to his rule. It was not in consequence of any official post that he could do this, but because he had won for himself a position of recognised supremacy in the assembly. A προστάτης who failed, who had no advice to give, who could not make a plausible speech, would thereby lose his position. He would not have to be ejected, he would

not lose it at an election; it would be *ipso facto*
forfeited to some successful rival[1].

This system had nothing irregular or informal *Constitu-*
about it. The orators when they undertook this *tional*
position
duty were perfectly aware that they were fulfilling *of the*
a public function, and had a full sense of the re- *orators.*
sponsibility attaching to it. What else is the
meaning of the law that a man shall be subject
to impeachment (εἰσαγγελία) because he has given
bad advice to the city[2]? In most states the responsibility for the mistakes of government belongs to
some official. At Athens it belonged to the man who
proposed the decrees which gave effect to the policy.
It was right and necessary that it should. A man
who proposed to enter on a war, or to found a colony,
or to remit a tax, was quite fairly held to be responsible for the result of his proposal, though he
had no official position. The law was no doubt often
abused: but it was none the less wise to establish
the principle that a man who of his own accord, to
justify his own ambition, put himself forward to
recommend a course of action should be held himself

---

[1] It is only necessary to read the Memorabilia to see how
futile is the attempt to find some elected official. The object of
political ambition is always represented as "προστατεύειν τοῦ δήμου,"
"ἐπιμελεῖσθαι τῶν δημοσίων." The two terms are used as identical
(ii. 8. 4, iii. 7. 1, iii. 6), and in connection with them Socrates never
makes any reference to elections. The prize is always attained by
coming forward as a speaker in the Assembly. But whenever he
mentions the generals he always has some reference to election
(iii. 1. 4, iii. 4. 1). Had there been any finance office which was
an object of ambition, we must have had constant references
to it.

[2] Hypereides iii. 45—6.†

responsible for the result of his advice[1]. The advice
of the orators was not always good: it was often
very bad; the fact that the position of a προστάτης
was so powerful while it lasted, and yet so precarious,
was a great source of temptation; but at any rate
the state did not suffer from want of advice: the
absence of a financial Secretary did not mean neglect of the finance, or the absence of proper control.

Result of this system. How did this system work? Was it successful?
Did not the Athenian state suffer from the absence
of a single head to the financial system? The answer
is generally unfavourable. The eventual ruin of
Athens is represented as due to financial mismanagement. That it was to a great extent due to
pecuniary embarrassment, is certainly true. The
facts indeed seem to be as follows. The complete
Athenian system grew up at a time when the
population of Athens was small; when the amount
of personal property was moderate, and the difference
between the wealth of rich and poor in consequence
slight; while, at the same time, the wealth of the
city itself, owing to the large tribute of the allies,
was, in proportion to the wealth of other cities, very
great. There was therefore no difficulty in getting
the money necessary for carrying on the government; the ordinary expenses were small, and of
these the greater part was met by the system of

---

[1] Dinarchus in Dem. 35 illustrates the duties of a leading
orator; he puts a series of questions, "ἔγραψάς τι —συνεβούλευσας—
ἐπόρισας χρήματα; A man who had once come forward was expected
and required to continue his activity just as much as if he were an
official.

λῃτουργίαι. Under these circumstances finance administration was easy. It was not difficult to provide the necessary money, and there was no need for the exercise of particular ingenuity in the levying of taxes.

In the 4th century the circumstances had altered. *Financial* The chief sources of the income of the state were *decline of Athens.* gone; and at the same time the expenses had greatly increased. The use of mercenary soldiers was a constant drain on the resources of the state. At the same time the increasing commercial prosperity of Athens, which does not seem to have been permanently affected by her political disasters, produced a complete change in her social conditions. The old hereditary landed aristocracy was extinct: their place was taken by wealthy capitalists, merchants, and shipowners; and with the capitalist appears the pauper; there are found a considerable number of citizens who have not sufficient to support themselves[1]. The result of this was that financial questions assumed a difficulty from which they had before been free. It became now a serious question how sufficient money could be raised for public purposes in such a way as to cause least discontent. The incidence of taxation was an important point: if a war was imminent, the first question to be decided was whether the money to carry it on was available, and whence it was to be obtained. On the decision of this question depended the safety of

[1] Cf. Isocrates, Areopagiticus, 83 νῦν πλείους εἰσὶν οἱ σπανίζοντες τῶν ἐχόντων.

Cf. also περὶ εἰρήνης 127—8.

the state, and the manner in which the money was raised might cause the ruin of a whole class of citizens. Hence arose the necessity for having a specialist at the head of the finances: altered conditions required a change in the constitution; the democratic institutions had suited the conditions of which the democracy was itself a product, but they were no longer equal to the strain when a large mercantile city which carried on its wars by mercenaries, in which all expenses had to be met by direct taxation, was pitted against a king who had behind him all the resources of a continental nation, and possessed the richest gold mines of the ancient world.

The change in the constitution had begun. The institution of the ἐπὶ τῇ διοικήσει, and the position held by the ἐπὶ τὸ θεωρικόν, are a sign that the council and orators were no longer equal to the work which they had formerly done; and a change had almost imperceptibly come over the administration, which, had Athens been victorious in the war with Philip, would have led as surely to an overthrow of the old constitution as did the victory of the Macedonians. With the increase of education and the increase of wealth, the government would have tended to pass into the hands of the wealthy merchant; the new elective offices would have overshadowed the old which were filled by lot; the council of 500 would have lost its power, or changed the mode of election; Athens would have become a democracy after the type of Rhodes. The assembly might have kept its sovereign power, but

the direct government of the city must have passed
out of its hands. This would have been so because
the circumstances which rendered the complete democracy possible were unique. A successful government always expresses the social condition of the
people. The use of the lot was only possible owing
to the compactness and homogeneity of the Athenian
population. When the increase of wealth had divided
Athens into two cities, the city of the rich and city
of the poor, it became an anachronism.

§ 2. *Subordinate Administration.*

The supreme control of the finance was then the
duty of the orators acting as advisers to the assembly;
but if all questions were there debated, and if all
speakers had to be acquainted with these matters,
the detailed administration must have been of such
a kind as to make it easy to get an insight into the
financial condition of the city. How this was done
we must now enquire.

The administration was the function of the *Duties of*
council and the subordinate offices. The relation of *the Council.*
the council and assembly was in this the same as in
all other matters. The council had no independent
power; it was only the committee of the assembly,
whose duty was to bring into order the mass of details which would otherwise have interfered with its
freedom of action. In finance, inasmuch as here
so much depends on accuracy of detail, the duties of
the council were more extended, and those of the
assembly smaller than in other departments. The

ordinary income of the state came from the sale of taxes, the letting of public lands and mines, and a number of smaller dues, fines, etc. These having been in the first instance paid to the κληρωτοί officials (of whom more presently), they, as soon as the money was received, paid it in to the ἀποδεκταί, who received it in the βουλευτήριον in the presence of the council, or more strictly of the πρυτάνεις. The money thus passed into the possession of the state; but the central bureau was not presided over by a single man, but by the 500 councillors. If the money were wanted for immediate use it would then probably be at once paid out by the ἀποδεκταί to the heads of the departments which required it; to the θεσμο-θέται, or to the στρατηγοί and ἀθλοθέται. Once a month the πρυτάνεις had to deliver before the ἐκκλησία an exact account of all moneys received † and expended by them during this period[1]. It is in this monthly account given by the πρυτάνεις to the ἐκκλησία that we must first look for the basis of the supreme finance administration, because in it would be apparent whether the receipts exceeded the necessities of the time, or whether there was a deficit. It was by a comparison of these published accounts, month by month, and year by year, that politicians would get the information they desired. It was there that the summary of the expenses of the time was to be found. It was by means of these accounts that surplus or deficit became apparent. This, therefore, was the mode in which the

[1] Cf. Gilbert, St. I. p. 323.

people were kept informed as to the condition of the public exchequer.

The council was moreover the intermediate body which tabulated the requirements of each department, in order that they might be easily explained to the assembly, and it was the council who were responsible for calling attention to any necessary changes. Suppose on any occasion the income did not suffice for the expenditure—that the proceeds of the mines were not sufficient to pay for the building of new triremes, or the other taxes did not bring in enough to pay for the $\delta\iota\omega\beta\epsilon\lambda\iota a$. The $\tau\rho\iota\eta\rho\sigma\pi\sigma\iota\sigma\iota$ or $\theta\epsilon\sigma\mu\sigma\theta\epsilon\tau\alpha\iota$ would as usual apply to the council for the money which they required to build the ships, or give the two obols at the festival; but the council had not the money: either the expenses had increased, or owing to disasters at sea the income had diminished. It rested with the council to meet the difficulty, for they were responsible to the assembly, and would be called to account if the triremes were left unbuilt, or the two obols not paid. But they had no power themselves to raise new taxes, and there was no large reserve fund of which they had the disposal. Their only method of action would be to come before the assembly, and there announce the deficit. The orators would thereupon propose means of relief. Many suggestions would be made; a full discussion might take place on the financial condition of the city; but if the $\pi\rho\sigma$-$\sigma\tau\acute{a}\tau\eta s$ of the time had a strong position, the assembly would accept his advice and act on his policy. This was doubtless the procedure in the case of the loans from the sacred treasure of which we have record. During the rule of Pericles, and throughout the Peloponnesian war, the tribute was often not sufficient to meet the extraordinary expenses. The στρατηγοί, the ἀθλοθέται, the θεσμοθέται found themselves without the necessary supplies; they gave notice to the council; the πρυτάνεις, probably after enquiry, brought the matter before the assembly, and the proposal was made to raise the money by borrowing from the sacred treasures. During the Peloponnesian war of course this was often necessary. It had become customary to meet a great number of the regular expenses of the state by charging them on the proceeds of the tribute paid by the allies, which were under the charge of the Hellenotamiai. When owing to the revolt or poverty of the allies the tribute failed, either the Generals or the Hellenotamiai would report to the council that there was no longer money to make the usual payments. The council reported to the assembly. The assembly decided (probably by the advice of the leading orator of the time) that money should be paid in to the Hellenotamiai from the treasure stored in the temples.

The council chamber thus formed the central bureau, from which direction and control could be exercised over all departments; and all payments were made by the Prytanies, sitting as the representatives of the people, through their clerks the ἀποδεκταί, a body of men appointed annually by lot.

The monthly accounts which had to be laid

before the assembly were probably drawn up by the
Prytanies themselves or their "secretary" (γραμματεύς), unless—as is possible—this was one of the
duties of the Logistai.

These Logistai were a board of 30 men, who were *Logistai.* †
appointed by lot. They were the public accountants
of the state. The monthly accounts of the Prytanies,
though they afforded a means of comparing the total
income and expenditure for the month, and would
ordinarily prevent any extensive fraud on the part
of the members of the council, would yet have to be
much supplemented if the orators and politicians
were to possess the information necessary for preparing financial schemes, and getting a grasp of
the condition of affairs. It was the duty of the
Logistai, at the command of the council or assembly,
to supplement these, as often as was desired, by
preparing tables of statistics. Whenever a statement was required of the total expenses of any
department, or of the debts of the state, or the
produce of a tax, application would be made to the
Logistai, who had then to produce the information.

This duty was of most consequence at the annual
examination of the retiring magistrates, and at the
quadrennial examination of all the public accounts.
Every magistrate, before he retired from office, had to
produce an account of all the public money of which
he had had charge. It was the duty of the Logistai,
as public accountants, to examine these accounts;
and to test their accuracy by comparing them with
one another. If in the accounts of the Treasurers of
the Goddess, or the Hellenotamiai, a sum was entered

as paid to the Generals, the Logistai would have to turn to the accounts published by the Generals to see whether this sum was properly entered there. Similarly, the accounts of the Poletai would be checked by a comparison with those of the Practores, from whom they had received the confiscated property of public debtors, and of the various companies who had bought from them any tax. Supposing any inaccuracy were discovered, this could be made the ground for legal proceedings; and, according to the regular Attic custom, the case would be tried by a jury court presided over by the Logistai.

The duties of the Logistai were however in no way confined to this audit. Whenever any statistical information concerning the finances was desired, the council or assembly would require the Logistai to produce it. Hence the Logisterion was a kind of archive house, where were kept not only the accounts of each board of magistrates, but financial statements of all kinds which had been drawn up by the Logistai. Some of these have been preserved to us.

During the Peloponnesian war, the ταμίαι τῆς θεοῦ were ordered to pay from the treasure under their charge certain sums of money to the Generals and other officials, in order to meet the deficit caused by the failure of the tribute and the expenses of the war. In order simply to test the correctness of the accounts, it would have been sufficient to see that the sum entered by the ταμίαι as paid corresponded to that which the Generals and other officials professed to have received. But the money was only borrowed from the temples: it would have to be repaid, and repaid with interest; but as it would be repaid not by the separate boards to which it had been lent, but by the council from the general fund at their disposal, it was necessary to have a record of the whole sum borrowed, together with the interest on it. The treasurers, as representatives of the Goddess to whom the money was owed, would doubtless keep such a record; but the state which owed the money would also have to do so. We have the fragments of a table of this kind, which has been drawn up by the Logistai as a record of the money owed to the Goddess by the state[1].

If the supposition be correct, according to which the lists of the firstfruits of tribute due to Athene were drawn up by the 30 Logistai, we get in these another instance of the same kind[2]. The tribute paid each year varied to some extent, and so oι course the sum received by the temple treasure also varied: in order therefore to be able at any time to know what sum had been paid, the λογισταί themselves kept a full list of the amount of the firstfruits. Each successive board of λογισταί as they came into office would find a full statement of what money had been paid into the Treasury. This they would use for reference in the quadrennial examination of the temple accounts; and it would also be available

---

[1] C. I. A. i. 273.

[2] C. I. A. i. 226—254. These lists are put up ὑπὸ τῶν τριά-κοντα, who are probably the same as οἱ λογισταί οἱ τριάκοντα of C. I. A. i. 32.

whenever, for the discussion of financial matters, a statement of the money in the temples and the probable income for future years was necessary. Similarly, when the council was occupied with the question of the assessment of the allies, the help of the Logistai would be required. The total sum to be exacted from the allies having been fixed by the assembly, it was the duty of the council to determine each year the quota to be paid by each city. It is surely not unreasonable to suppose that the help of the Logistai, and the tables drawn up by them, would be used in order to make the necessary calculations.

Another instance is preserved in an inscription, which records the repayment of a certain sum of money that was owed to the sacred treasures. In it we find that the council is ordered to summon the Logistai, who are to calculate the sum which is to be repaid, and make a report to the council[1].

In all these cases we see that, though the existence of these documents would make fraud by the officials very difficult, this was not their only value. They would make it possible for anyone to acquire with very little difficulty an accurate knowledge of the financial condition of the city. By going to the Logisterion, any citizen could in a short time at first hand get the information which Socrates warned Glaucon was necessary for all who wished to give the city useful advice. The people would learn that without which they could not manage their own affairs. The publicity of business was secured.

It is surprising to us that the Athenians should

[1] C. I. A. i. 32.

have considered this to be work which did not require special skill, and could be entrusted to men selected by lot. With regard to them we should especially like to know from what class of the population they were generally taken; also whether they always sat and worked all together, or were divided into several separate divisions each of which took part of the work. We can at least be sure that the fact that so many men were together responsible for the work, and that they were appointed only for one year by lot would completely avert what is for such a body the most serious danger, that of collusion. Appointed as they were, any deliberate agreement with the other magistrates, whether treasurers or executive, would be almost impossible; and the remains which we possess are sufficient to show that their work was thoroughly done[1].

We can now pass on to the consideration of ἀποδεκταί. the duties of others of the officials. The ἀποδεκταί I have already mentioned. They appear to have been little more than clerks. They sat in the council chamber, received money when it was paid in, counted it, gave receipts, paid it out, and took receipts. The only question concerning them which presents much difficulty is whether they had a treasury of their own where money was kept. Supposing money were paid in to the ἀποδεκταί which

---

[1] For a case where the work was dishonestly done, cf. Aesch. in Tim. 107 (126), λογιστὴς γὰρ γενόμενος πλεῖστα μὲν τὴν πόλιν ἔβλαψε δῶρα λαμβάνων παρὰ τῶν οὐ δικαίως ἀρξάντων, μάλιστα δ' ἐσυκοφάντησε τοὺς μηδὲν ἠδικηκότας.

H.   9

was not at once wanted by some other office, but
would be wanted for the current expenses, and so
could not be added permanently to the reserve fund,
what would be done with it? where was it kept?
would it even for one night be added to the sums
kept in the ὀπισθόδομος, or was there some treasure-
house under the immediate control of the council?
We must, I think, assume that there was, but, so far
as I know, no record of it has been preserved[1].

† κωλακρέ-
ται.

A point of some interest is the relation of the
ἀποδεκταί to the κωλακρέται[2]. All we are able to
make out is, that the latter was a very old office;
while the ἀποδεκταί were most likely introduced
either by Cleisthenes, or later, for they are closely
connected with the council of the 500, and were
probably first created when it acquired its administrative duties. The κωλακρέται were however retained for some time, and money for certain purposes
was paid by them till the end of the 5th century,
after which they seem to disappear. They are said
generally to have paid money for sacred and ritual
purposes, but in the inscriptions this is not ex-

---

[1] We hear of a ταμίας τῆς βουλῆς, but probably his duties were
quite unconnected with the control exercised by the βουλή over the
expenses of the State. He had charge of the fund which the
council required for its own expenses,—to pay its messengers
and slaves, to provide for the setting up of decrees, etc. This must
be clearly distinguished from the administration of the unappro-
priated public money.

[2] Harpocr. ad voc. ἀποδεκταί says:—ὅτι δὲ ἀντὶ τῶν κωλακρετῶν
οἱ ἀποδεκταὶ ὑπὸ Κλεισθένους ἀπεδείχθησαν, Ἀνδροτιῶν ἐν τῷ δευτέρῳ.
The κωλακρέται are however constantly mentioned in inscriptions
throughout the 5th century.

clusively the case[1]. It is disappointing that we are not told how the κωλακρέται were appointed: it would be a considerable help to know in what way the Athenians dealt with an old-established semi-religious office of this kind.

The Logistai and Apodectai were both closely connected with the council. They belonged to the central administration of the finances. We must now turn our attention to other officials who were occupied with the work of the various departments.

And of these it will be convenient first to take ἐλληνοτα-† the Hellenotamiai, because at one time their duties μίαι. became so extensive as to make them really treasurers of almost all the public money. We are unfortunately however left in ignorance on many points connected with them. There is even no record as to the manner and conditions of their appointment. This is due to the fact that, as they ceased to exist after the 5th century, the lexicographers tell us nothing of them. From the lists of them which are preserved we find however that they were probably 10 in number; that they were taken apparently from the wealthier classes; that the office was an annual one; and that re-election was not practised. Whether they were appointed by lot we do not know. The probability seems to be that they were: at least their duties do not seem to have been

---

[1] C. I. A. i. 25, iv. 11b, 27b, 35b, 53a. Schol. ad Aristoph. Vespae 695, Aves 1541. It seems as if they gradually lost their functions, since in some of the inscriptions quoted they pay money which in later times would be paid by the ἀποδεκταί. In the last they and the ἀποδεκταί are both mentioned.

of a different kind from those generally entrusted to the magistrates who were so elected. They were responsible for the custody of the tribute paid by the allies; they had to receive it from the collectors, acknowledge the receipt, and take care of it, till they received an order from the Assembly to pay it away. This work is exactly similar to that done by the Treasurers of the Goddess who, we know, were chosen by lot from among the members of the first class[1].

At the beginning of the Peloponnesian war the office of the Hellenotamiai had become the centre of the whole financial administration. The reason of this was that as the tribute of the allies was by far the largest sum which was. at the disposal of the Assembly, it had become customary to defray from it expenses which ought really to have been charged to other funds, and thus it happened that during the war, when the Treasurers of the Goddess advanced money to the state, they generally paid it to the Hellenotamiai. This was simply for convenience of management. The Generals, the Thesmothetai, and the Priests had been accustomed to draw their supplies from the Hellenotamiai. When their treasure was exhausted, the question how to provide money again came before the council and the Assembly. It was decided to have recourse to the sacred treasure, and the Treasurers were simply ordered to pay the money to the Hellenotamiai. The executive magistrates continued as before to

---

[1] It is common to say that the Hellenotamiai were elected, but I find no authority for this. Cf. Busolt in Müller's Handbuch, iv. 1. § 178.

draw upon them: and it was much easier to keep a
record of the public state if this money was paid
first into the treasure, and not direct to the several
departments.

Next in importance are the "Treasurers of the ταμίαι τῆς
Goddess." Our information about these is consider- θεοῦ.
able and of such a kind as to enable us to realise
with some detail the workings of the system of which
they formed a part. It is necessary to say however
that they stood on rather a different footing from
the other officials who were elected by lot, because,
according to an authority[1] whom there is no reason
for rejecting, they were not chosen from all citizens
but only from those who possessed sufficient property
to be classed among the πεντακοσιομέδιμνοι. The
reason of this was, apparently, that, supposing any of
the money entrusted to them disappeared, it might
be possible to recover it from the private property of
the treasurers. With this exception they seem to
have held a position similar to that of other κληρωταὶ
ἀρχαί, and their duties appear to have been strictly
defined in the way which was necessary for officials
so chosen[2].

Their actual business was the custody of the
money and treasure deposited in the temple on the
Acropolis. They had to take care that it was not
stolen[3]. The state had to see that the treasurers

---

[1] Pollux 8. 97; and Suidas referred to by Gilbert, St. I. p. 234.
[But see Appendix.]

[2] The first mention of them is in Herodot. viii. 51.

[3] Cf. Dem. in Timocratem 136 for a case where the ταμίαι were
accused of criminal negligence because the temple had caught fire.

themselves did not steal it. We find that ample means
were taken to ensure the attainment of both these
ends. Each board when it came into office had to
make a full inventory of all the treasures contained
in the temple, which on their retirement was handed
over to their successors. These after making their
own inventory would proceed to compare the
list of treasure actually present in the temple with
the list they had received. The treasurers might not
spend any money, nor part with any treasure (except
perhaps small sums) without the sanction of a special
vote of the assembly[1]; a special record of all such
authorised expenditure was made out by the treasurers. At the end of every four years the accounts
for that period were examined by the λογισταί: and
had any of the ταμίαι for any year abstracted aught
of the treasure, or owing to carelessness allowed it
to be taken, it would be impossible to avoid detection. If he had taken something away and omitted
it on the list he handed over to his successors, the
fraud would at once be discovered by a comparison
of his list with that of his predecessor: and, unless
he could show some decree authorising him to take
it away, or some other public body to whom he had
paid the money (in which case the receipt of it
would have been entered in the accounts of that
body in the possession of the λογισταί), he would
have to make good the loss to the state, and be
liable to a criminal prosecution. On the other hand,
supposing he abstracted something, but entered the

---

[1] Cf. C. I. A. i. 188, v. 3, ψηφισαμένου τοῦ δήμου. In l. c. 183—4
we find the formula ψηφισαμένου τοῦ δήμου τὴν ἄδειαν.

money or treasure in his list as though it were still there, the loss would be discovered by his successors when they made up their list. The advantage of the collegiate system, annual office, and election by lot will be clear. Peculation or fraud could only be successful if the officials several years together entered into a conspiracy, for it was the officials of one year who in self-defence were obliged to point out any mistakes in the accounts of their predecessors. But a conspiracy of the extent which would have been necessary must have been almost impossible, just because the officials of each year were bound together by no tie; that they served together was pure chance; and no board could foresee by whom it would be succeeded. Had there been one or two ταμίαι, had they been elected, had re-election been allowed, or had the office been held for many years, then peculation would have been possible and comparatively easy; because there would have been fewer persons involved, and there would have been more time. Had the λογισταί been few in number, had they been elected, there might have been a hope of bribing them and giving them a share of the profits, or of getting suitable people elected. To admit 30 men chosen by chance into a conspiracy of the kind would only have been possible where public morality and public spirit were very low. Had that been the case, the democracy could not have existed[1]. What it required was a good deal of public

---

[1] Aeschines in Timarchum 109 etc. (127—28) relates an instance where a ταμίας was enabled to steal money from the temple by the collusion of a βουλευτής, but he does not say any-

activity, and a moderate standard of honesty; what
the constitution ensured was that the officials should
not have any temptation to fall below the average of
honesty—a temptation which is often present, and
perhaps seldom resisted. The object of all such
machinery must be not to raise the standard of
probity, but to make use of it, and to apply it to
the public administration.

The inscriptions which have been discovered are
sufficient to convince us of the reality of the precautions taken, and of the care devoted to the
arrangement of all the details of the system. The
most interesting is one[1] which records a vote of the
ἐκκλησία concerning the creation of a new board of
treasurers, apparently those which were known as the
ταμίαι τῶν ἄλλων θεῶν. This shows us clearly the
working of the system. The whole arrangements
are made by a decree of the Assembly; it is the
δῆμος which decides that the money shall be repaid
to the gods, and sets apart a certain revenue to meet
the expenditure. The work is entirely carried out
by men elected by lot: first of all, the λογισταί
calculate exactly what the sum due is; then, when
they have done so, the money has to be paid back to
the priests and other officials, from whom it had
been borrowed, by the Prytanies in the council; and
all the documents in possession of the priests re-
cording the debt are to be destroyed. By this

thing which enables one to see how he did it. The difficulty in
this and similar cases is that we do not know how much members
of the board could do alone without their colleagues.

    [1] C. I. A. i. 32. Hicks N. 38.†

means the account with the priests and curators will be closed. The decree then proceeds to make arrangements for the custody of the money in the future. Treasurers are to be chosen by lot, the priests and curators (who have just received the money) are then to pay it to the new board in the presence of the council. The new treasurers are then to count it, and publish a list of what they have in their possession; and every year the board has similarly to publish a list of the money in the treasury, with an account of all which they have received or spent.

This decree is in many ways very remarkable. It was made in the year 435. Pericles' influence was then at its height, and we may naturally suppose, even if the actual wording be not his, that it expresses his policy. It was passed after the full democratic constitution had been introduced; all the officials mentioned in it are elected by lot. A careful examination of it will, I think, bear out the position I am defending, that efficiency of administration was one of the chief characteristics of the Democratic constitution of which election by lot was a part. The framers of the decree have a distinct end in view, and they have an ample machinery to attain it; the wording of the decree is simple and straightforward, it is not burdened with circumlocutions, there is no parade of legal accuracy, but at the same time the meaning of each clause is quite clear[1]. For the execution of the

[1] There is an almost pedantic adherence to the proper forms: the money is to be paid by the πρυτάνεις to the old ἱερεῖς, i.e. the

decree a number of officials are required, but the
duties of each are carefully defined, and every precaution is taken to make it clear that each board
has one definite thing to do, which it must do, and
no more. The execution of the whole depends on
the efficient co-operation of a number of men, but
their duties do not overlap. The duties assigned to
each are in fact so simple only because they belong
to a highly organised system. Election by lot appears here not as the result of democratic jealousy,
but as part of a clearly thought-out system, which
has been carefully elaborated so as to exclude as far
as possible serious mismanagement, or fraud. The
Athenian intellect applying itself to financial organisation has produced a system which shows admirable
clearness of conception and thoroughness of execution. It is possible that the system was not so
perfect in its working as it appears to be on paper:
but this decree at least justifies us in maintaining
that the statesmen who introduced the lot did not
do so recklessly; one is tempted to think that one
of the chief reasons why Pericles made his democratic
changes was that he saw in them the only means of
getting a pure and efficient administration.

πωληταί.   Among other officials who were connected with
finance were the Poletai: that they were appointed
by lot illustrates the remarkable nature of the system.
They had to transact on the part of the state all the
business connected with the sale of any public

officials from whom it was borrowed: and then is paid by them to
the new ταμίαι: not paid direct by the πρυτάνεις to the new
ταμίαι.   Cf. vv. 10 and 18.

property, and the reception of tenders from contractors for the execution of public works. Their
office was of particular importance because among
their duties was the sale of the taxes to the men
who farmed them. From this alone it follows that a
very large part of the permanent income of the State
must have passed through their hands. Besides this,
they dealt with all the money which came from the
sale of property which had been confiscated. Now
this, especially in times of distress, was no in-
considerable sum, and the proceeds of such sales
were looked on as an important part of the public
income.

The duties would be the registration and publication of all taxes, contracts, and property which was
to be sold. The publication took place by notices
put up outside the office of the Poletai in the
Agora[1]. Here too the actual sale would generally
take place. In the case however of important
taxes, it appears that the sale took place before the
council[2]; and it is not improbable that the members
of the council actually voted as to who should be
allowed to buy the tax; a procedure analogous to
that which sometimes took place in the lease of the
property of a minor by the Archons in a law-court.
In less important matters where this did not happen,
the sale was by public auction. Probably the ten
Poletai sat on raised seats and presided; the pro-
clamations would be made by a Herald, and the
Secretary of the board would take notes of the

---

[1] Cf. Wachsmuth, Die Stadt Athen, ii. 357.
[2] Andoc. de mysteriis, 132—134. [See Appendix.]

proceedings. The Poletai would be responsible that
all was done with proper formality; they would
determine on the time, see that due notice was
served, give the necessary orders to the public slaves,
and formally assign the purchase to the highest
bidder[1]. For the preservation of order there would
be one or more police (τοξόται) at their disposal.
The purchaser would then have to pay the money
to the Poletai in their office; after which, they would
personally hand over the property, or in some form
give a certificate of purchase. Finally, they had at
once to pay the money which they had received to
the Apodectai in the Bouleuterion; and, when the
year was over, to draw up and publish accounts of
all they had received by sales. These would at the
end of their office be examined by the Logistai, and
would afterwards be preserved among the other
archives[2].

πράκτορες.   It is not possible to get quite as clear a picture
of the duties of the Practores. They had to exact
the money from men who had been fined by a
magistrate, or by a law-court. The magistrate who
had inflicted the fine, or the president of the court,
sent a record of it to the πράκτορες, who, we must
suppose, had also a regular office. They would then
either by means of a public slave, or in person,
request payment. If the fine were paid at once,
the record of the debt would be destroyed, and
the Practores would hand over the money to the

---

[1] Plutarch, Alc. v.

[2] There are preserved several fragments of inscriptions which
appear to belong to these accounts of the Poletai. C. I. A. i. 274, etc.†

Apodectai. If payment were delayed, the name of the defaulter would be entered in the list of public debtors, the supervision of which was the chief duty of these officials, and until his name was erased the defaulting debtor would be deprived of his political privileges. If the debt were in any way disputed, the matter could be made the subject of a fresh trial; and in that case the Practores would empanel a jury, and themselves preside in the court. If however a debtor from want of money did not pay the debt, he seems generally to have been left at large, but was liable to a criminal prosecution supposing he attempted to use his rights as a citizen. If for any reason rigorous measures were to be adopted, the Practores would order the confiscation of his property; which would then be handed over to the Poletai to be sold. If it were movable, the Practores would request the Eleven to go and seize it. In some cases the person of the debtor would be seized, and he would be kept in prison. The names of men who had not paid the taxes would also be given to the Practores as public debtors, but probably only after they had been convicted in court. The duties of the office seem however to have been chiefly the collection of debts in consequence of the decision of a court, and the care of the list. Their duties, important as they were, were only a single part in the procedure by which money from condemned criminals was safely conveyed to the public treasury. The principle of division of labour is here also carried out. This careful limitation of the duties of each office, which in a modern bureaucracy is often so deadening, was necessary when the officials were changed each year.

These πράκτορες were closely connected in their duties with the Eleven.

The Eleven.   The Eleven seems to have been an euphemistic name for officials who in later times and in other states were called δεσμοφύλακες[1]. They had not only the charge and control of the prisons, with the duty of superintending and being present at public executions, but they had also to seize the persons of men who were to be imprisoned and the property which had been confiscated. The actual taking into custody and execution was of course performed either by slaves or servants.

From the account of the death of Socrates given by Plato, we learn that the whole college of the Eleven announced to him personally the approach of his death. It is probable that a distinguished prisoner like Socrates would be treated with more respect than an ordinary man who was to be executed; but this narrative will remind us that the dignity of these offices, which might easily have suffered from the mode of appointment, would be preserved by the number of members of which they consisted. They would give countenance and authority to one another: whether it were the Poletai presiding at a sale, the Eleven at an execution, or the Practores in court, an ordinary citizen who would have no respect

---

[1] It was probably from a similar feeling that the prison was generally called τὸ οἴκημα. Cf. Wachsmuth, l. c. ii. p. 383, n. 2. They are also called ἐπιμεληταὶ τῶν κακούργων. Antiphon, de morte Herodis, § 17.†

for one of these men individually would be quicker
to recognise in them the authority of the laws when
he saw them moving about together and acting in
company. This is not necessary when the magistrates are members of one class in the state; or when,
being appointed for their ability and holding office
for many years, they can gather around their own
persons the mystery and dignity of office. The corporate and collective action of many men, however
foolish and insignificant as individuals, would form
some substitute for this.

The εἰσφορά, or direct property tax, which was *Other
Officials.*
only levied in times of war, or other great necessity,
was not sold as were the indirect taxes. It was
collected directly by the state. For the collections
there were special officers appointed. We hear of
διαγραφεῖς, who had apparently to superintend the
assessment, and ἐκλογεῖς, who actually collected it.
These latter are said by the lexicographers to have
been chosen by lot, and this statement is supported
by a passage in Demosthenes[1]. If this be the case,
they are an exception to the rule that men were
never chosen by lot for any but continuous offices;
unless indeed, as is possible, they were appointed
annually, so that all the machinery might be ready
for the levying of a tax should one be required. We
have no information about them, and it is probable
that both in the formation of the register and the
collection of the money, the officials of the Demes
and other divisions did the greater part of the

[1] Androtion 48. The ἐπιγραφεῖς, however, mentioned by Isocrates xvii. 41 were elected.

work, which would otherwise have been far more than could have been managed by a single board. The διαγραφεῖς and ἐκλογεῖς must have superintended the action of the local officials on behalf of the central government.

This list of officials will give some conception of the wealth of labour spent by the Athenians on a single part of their administration; and it illustrates the chief characteristics of the system. The work was so much divided, that the duties of each office were very simple. In consequence, it was possible to fix the responsibility for any neglect of duty, or dishonesty, upon the board in whose jurisdiction the matter was; and an elaborate system of accountability resulted, by which it was the interest of any one office to point out the dishonesty of another, and whereby it became difficult to organise any fraud without the certainty of detection. It does not sound a great deal to say that the Athenian system rendered it difficult for its officials to cheat, and made it clear with whom the responsibility for doing any particular thing rested; but a very slight knowledge of the administration of ancient and modern states will remind us that most governments have not been able to attain what seems at first so easy.

CHAPTER V.

THE extension of the custom of election by lot to judicial offices is more remarkable than any other use of it. It will be necessary to examine the object and result of this shortly. It will also be interesting to see to what extent the method of election caused the peculiarities of the Athenian legal system.

It is unnecessary to dwell on the effect which the *Absence of class of trained lawyers.* existence of a class of trained lawyers has had on the constitutional development of various countries. Both in England and in Rome their decisions have had a great part in the creation of the laws; and in America it is the lawyers alone who are now to some extent removed from the influence of the popular will, and can even stop the execution of the laws passed by the representative assemblies. In these and in other cases we find a complicated system of law, administered by a class of men who have had a special training, and are strongly influenced by professional feeling. The complex system of law and the great influence of lawyers go together; one cannot exist without the other, and both are clearly

opposed to the influence of Democracy. Both of
these were completely unknown at Athens. This
is so obvious that it perhaps seems superfluous to
call attention to it; and yet it is worth while to
ask the reason of it, the more so as their absence
was essential to the existence of the Democracy.

At first sight there is very great resemblance
between the duties of a Roman Prætor and an
Athenian Archon. The great influence which the
Compari- Prætor had on the development of the Roman law
son of the came from duties which were nearly akin to those of
Archon
and the the Athenian Archons. In both cases the chief duty
Prætor. of the magistrate was not to try the case, but to
prepare it for trial; in both cases the actual trial
was before jurors: with this important distinction,
that at Rome civil cases were generally tried before
a single judex, at Athens before a large δικαστήριον.
At Athens as at Rome this arrangement was the
result of a historical development: the original
Archons like the original Prætors had themselves
heard and settled all cases, and it was only by a
later development that their duties were limited
as they were.

Schömann explains clearly what were the duties
of the Archon, or other official, under the system as
we know it[1]. It was before him that the plaintiff
and defendant in a suit had to appear: they had to
explain the grounds of the action, and had to collect
evidence and lay it before him. The duties of the

---

[1] Meier u. Schömann Attischer Process, ed. by Lipsius. Cp.
esp. 11. 41, etc.

magistrate were to a great extent formal, and would have been performed perfectly well by a clerk[1]. He made no comment, and gave no opinion. He simply entered the case on the lists of those to be tried, and decided on which day it should be heard. He was also responsible for summoning the jury. It was indeed possible that the plaintiff had come before the wrong court: he might have summoned an alien to appear before the Thesmothetai, instead of before the Polemarch. In this case the magistrate could point out the error, and dismiss the case. But his influence did not extend beyond this. He did not use his position to declare, or interpret the law. And it is in this that he differs from a Roman Prætor. When a case was brought forward in Rome, the Prætor listened to the evidence on both sides and himself formulated the plea, and he did so in such a manner as thereby to declare the law. He exercised moreover very wide discretion in accepting or rejecting a case. He could, and often did refuse to grant a trial either because the plea had no real legal basis, or—a more remarkable stretch of his authority—because it seemed to him that the legal

[1] The account of the duties of the magistrate, ch. II. pp. 42—44 compared with the account of the ἀνάκρισις p. 790 etc. makes it clear that the only matters which in any case were left to his decision were (1) whether he should receive the suit, (2) on what day the case should be tried. Of these, as to (1), he had little latitude allowed him; he could only refuse to receive a suit in cases where to do so would be an obvious contravention of a law. His other duties were to receive the evidence on both sides, hear the oaths taken, and put the case in proper order: but all as a clerk might do it.

claims on which it was founded conflicted with
equity.

*Small
powers
of the
Archon.*   But the Archon never used his personal judgment
in this way: he took on himself no responsibility of
this kind: it was inconceivable to an Athenian
that he should. All he could do was, when the
law clearly said that causes of a certain kind should
be brought before a certain magistrate and not
before him, to refuse to receive them. Suppose
there were a dispute as to the interpretation of this
law, even that the Archon or Thesmothetes did not
himself decide. It was made the ground of a separate
action and referred to a jury—in some cases referred
to the same jury who tried the whole case, so that
the same court had at the same time to consider the
merits of the plea, and its own competence to try it[1].

What is the cause of this difference? Clearly
this: that the Archons were chosen by lot, and the
Prætors elected. The Prætor was chosen to fill his
office either because of personal ability or because of
his birth. But if he was chosen because of his rank,
he was a member of a close body of men among
whom a great knowledge of law was common. The
leading lawyers were all Senators; a Senator did not
act independently, he acted as a member of his
order. A Prætor in his legal decisions would not
only be giving his own opinion, he would be the
mouthpiece of a body which contained all the legal

---

[1] Cf. Schömann l. c. p. 841 etc. In all the different forms
which he describes, διαμαρτυρία—παραγραφή—ἐξωμοσία, we find
that the question of jurisdiction is brought before a jury, and
not decided by a magistrate.

traditions and wisdom of the state. Hence his decisions would have authority; if the Prætor told a plaintiff that he had no case, and refused to grant an action, the plaintiff would feel that the law had spoken: he would know that the Prætor had consulted other men before giving his decision. And the decision of the Prætor in consequence formed a precedent; it would be incorporated in the Edict of his successor, and would become a substantive part of the law as administered.

But an Athenian Archon had no power to take upon himself to grant or refuse a suit. He represented no one, he was of no special ability or knowledge. Had he done so, his act would have been purely arbitrary; he would not himself have been bound to act in the same way in other cases, much less would his colleagues and successors have been influenced by it. He had therefore none of that power of indirect legislation which at Rome was in the hands of the legal profession. And so the duties which the Roman Prætor carried out with intelligence the Archon performed mechanically.

A single case will help to make this clear. After *Instance* the revolution of 403 an amnesty was passed, one *of this.* clause of which decreed that (with certain excep- *The παρα-* tions) political acts done before that date should not *γραφή.* be made the ground of a criminal prosecution. Of course, as could have been foreseen, attempts were made to evade this law, and difficulties arose as to the interpretation of it[1]. In consequence it often

---

[1] Cf. Isocrates, πρὸς Καλλίμαχον § 1—3.

happened that someone was accused of murder, and pleaded in his defence not only that he was innocent, but also that he was protected by the Amnesty. It was obviously inconvenient that these two completely different questions should be tried at the same time by the same court: how then was a plea of this kind to be met? It was as a rule one not of fact, but of law: "If the defendant has committed the murder, is it one of those crimes which come under the Amnesty, or not?" Had a similar case arisen in Rome, or in any other state where the magistrate had authority and influence as a man learned in the law, the Prætor himself would have decided it. He would have granted or refused an action, according as he thought the defendant was protected or not by the Amnesty. But at Athens the Archons never attempted to take this responsibility on themselves. The only way of escape was a Law. Hence a law was passed through the ἐκκλησία instituting a new form of procedure to meet this special case—the well-known παραγραφή[1]. A difficulty which at Rome would have been settled by the Prætor could at Athens not be solved without an appeal to the Assembly. We see at once how the power of the δῆμος was a direct result of the absence of ability and influence among the magistrates; in other words, how election by lot was necessary to the perfection of the democracy.

Characteristics of Athenian Law. We can now see to what was due the chief characteristic of the Athenian law, its great sim-

---

[1] Cf. Schömann p. 850, n. 234.

plicity. This did not come from any peculiarities
of the Greek mind. The Athenians were not inferior
to the Romans in their power of framing a system,
nor were they wanting in ability to analyse the basis
of law; yet the Athenian law never got beyond
the rudimentary state: it remained merely a list of
rules or precepts for conduct, with apparently little
attempt at scientific arrangement. The Athenian
courts were active, the number of cases tried was
immense, and the complexity of the issues often
considerable, and yet there was no authoritative
interpretation of the law; no glosses were collected
round the rules; the laws remained short simple
and straightforward. This is of course due partly
to the peculiar constitution of the law-courts; but
it is still more due to the absence of authority of the
magistrates. Owing to this, there was no attempt
made to distinguish between questions of law and
questions of fact. The same men decided both together. Each case came before the court in its
entirety, and when the verdict was given no one
could tell on what grounds it had been given. Hence
there could be no precedent. A precedent is only
possible when an authoritative exposition can be
given of the law, in such a way that it is applic-
able to other cases, apart from the particular circumstances which were the occasion of it. This could not
be done at Athens; for there was no authoritative
ruling of the Judge, or formula of the Prætor, and the
very nature of the courts prevented their decision
becoming a precedent. Again, there was no customary law: there was nothing to which an advocate could

appeal but the written laws, "the laws of Solon."
The speechmakers were the only people who were
professionally connected with the law, and advocates
are only of use in developing a system of law when
the court before which they plead is itself composed
of professional lawyers.

One result of this again is the peculiar nature of
the Athenian laws. They are as a rule the concise
statement of some general principle. They are put in
such a form that they can be understood and applied
by a court of laymen. Elaborately drawn up laws
full of technical phraseology which aim at covering
every possible case, are really much easier to apply
than the apparently simpler rules; but they can
only be used by trained minds and memories. At
Athens no one was specially trained. It was moreover the absence of any authoritative explanation of
the law which caused the Athenians to be so particular about their laws. Inconsistencies in the law
and obscurities of expression are not of great importance where the interpretation of the laws is the
professed occupation of a large and organised
body of able men. The law will eventually be
hidden and superseded by the interpretation, and
the goodness or badness of the law be of little
moment. At Athens, where each case had to be
decided by inexperienced people, any inconsistency
in the laws would destroy all confidence in the
justice of the courts, and so the activity which in
other countries is devoted to elaborating the law
and making it more complete, at Athens was spent
in simplifying and shortening it.

This department shows, I think, more clearly *Relation of the legal system to the democracy* than any other, how true it is that the power of the Assembly depended on the absence of special ability in the magistrates and officials; and why it was that election by lot was so essential to the democracy. A consideration of this will convince us how far all modern states are from being what a Greek would have called a democracy. It will be an interesting problem in the future to see to what extent consistent democrats will succeed in doing away with what they ought to consider their most formidable enemy—a class of trained lawyers.

CHAPTER VI.

ADMINISTRATIVE OFFICIALS.

Com-
mittees of
the As-
sembly and
council.
THE principles which prevailed in the finance administration were consistently carried out in all other parts of the public service. The immediate control over each department of the state and the responsibility for the proper management of every separate public institution was placed in the hands of a special board of 10 men annually appointed by lot. Each of these was constitutionally a committee of the Assembly, or the council, and it was by means of these committees that the larger bodies kept up their control over the innumerable details of public business. The actual work was done by public slaves and by contractors: the duties of these committees were normally to inspect and control the work, so as to ensure that it was properly done.

It is impossible to give an account of all of these committees. The system will be best explained by investigating a single department which may be taken as typical of the others.

† ἐπιμεληταὶ
τῶν
νεωρίων.
Among them, those of whom we have most knowledge, are the inspectors of the dockyards. I propose therefore to give a short account of their

duties. This will show better than anything else the
sort of work which these committees had to do; for
the duties of the ἐπιμεληταὶ τοῦ ἐμπορίου, and even
of the σιτοφύλακες, or the μετρονόμοι, and other
boards must have been to some extent like theirs.
That is, as I shall explain, they had to see that the
wishes and decrees of the people were carried out;
they had to exercise for the people the control and
superintendence over its servants and workmen; and
they had to report and bring to trial all who were
guilty of neglect of duty[1].

Each year there was appointed a board of men,
ἐπιμεληταὶ τῶν νεωρίων, as superintendents and
inspectors of the dockyards. We have no direct
information as to the method of their appointment,
but I think that we shall be justified in assuming
with Boeckh[2] on the analogy of all similar offices that
they were appointed by lot[3]. An examination of the
duties they had to perform will show that this is in
itself not improbable. Apart from this, we find by
the lists which we possess that they were ten in
number, and were chosen one from each tribe, and
that re-election if not impossible at least was very

---

[1] I am entirely indebted to Boeckh for my account of these
inspectors. His edition of the inscriptions containing their
reports and accounts, published as an appendix to his Staatshaushaltung der Athener, contains a great mass of information.
The inscriptions discovered since he wrote, which are now
published in the 2nd volume of the Corpus, add little to our
knowledge. I refer to Boeckh's edition by Roman numbers, but
always add the reference to the Corpus.†

[2] p. 48.

[3] C. I. A. i. 77 shows us that they existed in the 5th century.

rare. Not a single case occurs of which we have
knowledge; and, though our lists are very fragmentary, they contain at least enough names to
show that re-election, if it ever occurred, was a
great exception. I should incline to believe that it
was unknown.

Annual In-
spection.
The duties of these ἐπιμεληταί, as appears from
the inscriptions, were during their year of office to
make a full inspection of the dockyards, and draw up
a complete list of all the ships and fittings which
they contained; as well as to enter in it all ships
which were at sea, and any articles which were missing, together with the name of the person who was
responsible for replacing them. When the board
came into office at the beginning of the official year,
they received a list from the retiring board. It would
then be their duty to make a careful inspection of
the dockyards, and see whether the list was correct.
If anything which was entered in the στήλη was not
forthcoming, the retiring ἐπιμεληταί with their secretary (γραμματεύς) were responsible, and had to re-
place it; and it was the duty of the new board to
institute proceedings for the recovery of this as of
all other debts[1]. This inspection was probably a
work of considerable length: it went into great
detail; and all the fittings of each several ship had
to be examined. Besides the inspection, the chief
duty of the ἐπιμεληταί was the collection of out-

[1] C. I. A. ii. 811 (xv. xvi.) c. 166, τάδε ὀφείλουσιν οἱ τῶν
νεωρίων ἐπιμεληταὶ οἱ ἐπ᾽ Ἀντικλέους ἄρχοντος καὶ ὁ γραμματεὺς
αὐτῶν τῶν σκευῶν, ὧν γράψαντες εἰς τὴν στήλην οὐ παρέδοσαν ὄντα ἐν
τοῖς νεωρίοις.

standing debts. In all cases where anyone was in
debt to the dockyards, the ἐπιμελεταί had to institute proceedings, and if the debt were disputed they
were the presiding officers in the jury court which
tried the case.

Debts to the dockyards might arise in three ways: *Debts.*
either (1) the preceding ἐπιμελεταί had not handed
over everything which according to the accounts
ought to have been forthcoming[1]. (2) The trierarchs
returned a ship not in proper condition, or with
some of her furniture missing. (3) New materials
had not been delivered by the builders, or the
materials delivered were bad[2]. Of these two latter
cases I shall speak presently, but for the present it
is sufficient to point out that normally all debts of
which the ἐπιμελεταί had cognisance were for the
non-delivery of certain goods; and the suit was
properly for the recovery of the goods, or an equiva-
lent. The inspectors were responsible to the state.
They had at the end of their year of office either
to deliver over all goods to their successors in
good condition, or show that the state had received
a substitute. If in such a suit the defendant paid
the money, the sum was not paid to the inspectors,
but to the Apodectai. This is at any rate expressly
stated in many cases, and when it was paid to the
inspectors, they did not keep it in a fund of their own,

---

[1] l. c. 803, (x.) d. 4—13. Also Dem. in Androt. 63, where
Σάτυρος, an ἐπιμελητής, has to collect a large number of such
debts.

[2] l. c. 803 (x.) c. 128, Εὔθυνος had delivered oars which were
useless (ἀδόκιμοι). Cf. also 811 (xvi.) b. 164 etc.

but at once paid it into the state chest[1]. Hence
they had no direct responsibility for money, and in
drawing up a list of what was handed over to their
successors they had no money to enter.

The general inspection and the recovery of debts
were then the ordinary duties of the inspectors; but
if, as of course must have happened every year, any
triremes were to be put into commission, the inspectors had to take special account of these.

The proceedings were as follows. The Assembly
would decide to send an expedition of one or more
ships if not for actual warfare, then perhaps to
raise tribute, found a colony, protect the corn ships,
escort an embassy. The vote of the Assembly would
generally determine the number of vessels required,
and according to circumstances would go more or
less into details as to the fittings which were necessary[2]. Generally however the decree which ordered
the expedition to be sent out would commission the
council to look after all details[3]. The appointment
of the trierarchs rested with the generals, and then
it was the duty of the inspectors to hand over the
required number of ships to the trierarchs. They
had to see that each ship was fully fitted out, and
take a careful list of all which it contained. When
the expedition was over, the trierarchs had to deliver

---

[1] l. c. 803 (x.) d. 133, p. 212. ἐς τὸ βουλευτήριον—τοῖς ἀπο-
δεκταῖς. 809 (xiv.), d. 62 etc.

[2] l. c. 809 (xiv.) a. A special ψήφισμα orders that certain ships
should be provided with two additional ὑποζώματα. They were as
Boeckh points out "bound for the stormy Adriatic."

[3] Also elected officials (ἀποστολεῖς) could be appointed to help
in the work and supplement the inspectors.

up the ships again to the inspectors, and to make
good all loss and damage, except such as was due to
storms, or fighting. The published accounts contain
the record of a great number of debts, varying from
a whole ship to an oar, or a sail. If however the
ship had been damaged in battle, or during a storm,
(κατὰ πόλεμον, κατὰ χειμῶνα) the trierarch had not
to make good the loss. When this had happened, he
would report the matter to the inspectors; if they
accepted the statement, it would be so entered in the
annual account of their inspection; if not, the matter
might eventually be brought before a law-court, since
the inspectors would have to sue the trierarchs for
the debt. In one case[1], we find that a dispute of
this kind was brought before the Assembly, and a
special decree passed declaring that in a particular
case damage which had been done to certain ships
should be considered to be κατὰ πόλεμον, and that
in consequence the trierarchs should not be held
liable for the loss. The payments of the debts by
the trierarchs seem to have been very tardy[2]; they
were often allowed to run on for years. In a few
cases the debts were doubled.

These inspectors were thus a committee of the *Character*
people, whose duty it was to control the administra- *of their*
tion of the dockyards: they did not do anything *duties.*
themselves, and they had no power to order anything
to be done, but they had to see that all orders of the

[1] l. c. 809, d. 138 etc.

[2] l. c. 803, x. contains records of old debts paid by trierarchs; in
several cases the debt was not paid till after the death of the man
who had incurred it, when it was paid by his heirs.

Assembly and council were properly executed, and they had to keep a constant record of all which happened in the dockyards, so that information might be easily accessible when required. To take a special instance. If new triremes were required, the council would have to send to the office of the inspectors for information as to the exact number and condition of the triremes; they would ask what number were at sea, how many were seaworthy, and which would be likely soon to want repairs. Then, acting on the information given by the inspectors, the council or the Assembly would order new triremes to be built. This would be the work of the τριηροποιοί[1]. When the triremes had been built, they would be handed over by the τριηροποιοί to the inspectors; who would then make a complete inspection in order to see whether they had been built in accordance with the orders of the council, and whether the work was properly done. The result of this inspection would be entered in their annual report. If the work were badly done they would institute proceedings against the τριηροποιοί, or, if anything were missing, against their ταμίας. If, as would sometimes happen, the inspectors failed to call attention to any defect in the execution of the order, they would themselves be responsible, and proceedings would be instituted against them by the next board.

The inspectors, then, were appointed by the people to act as stewards or bailiffs. The people was the

[1] It is unfortunate that our knowledge of these officials is very small. [See Appendix.]

owner of a large business establishment; the inspectors had to do the work of superintendence over the workmen which the owner had not time to do himself. They were a committee of the Assembly, or council, who were appointed by lot because they represented the whole people. The whole of the demos could not go together to the dockyards to see that the new ships which had been ordered were properly built, so they deputed a few of their number to do so, and as a matter of course, as in all such committees, made the appointment by lot.

The duties of the ἐπιμεληταὶ τῶν νεωρίων were indeed such as could be perfectly well performed by any intelligent citizen. They presupposed, it is true, a certain knowledge of naval matters. The inspectors must know the difference between ταρροί, πηδάλια, and κλιμακίδες. They must be able to judge whether a trireme was returned by the trierarch in proper repair; and, at times, had to decide whether the oars supplied by the builders were in proper condition, or not. But knowledge of this kind was just the sort of knowledge which an ordinary Athenian citizen would possess, or at least could easily acquire. If he had never himself been to sea, he must have constantly been to the Piræus; the condition of the navy, improvements in the triremes, the conduct of trierarchs were among the subjects which would constantly come up for discussion in society, in the law-courts, and in the ἐκκλησία. And a man who was not a judge of the comparative merits of two triremes could still count how many holes there were in a sail, and see whether any ropes were wanting in the

H. 11

rigging. An inspection of the kind which was required from them could perfectly well be carried out in this way.

If then we can allow this, the advantages of making the appointment annual and choosing the inspectors · by lot are obvious. It was the best guarantee against fraud. If the appointment had been for a number of years, there would have been a great temptation to connivance by the inspectors with the people whom they had to look after. And had the office been elective, the rich trierarchs and rich contractors by using their influence at an election might, as has often been done since, have managed to procure the election of men who, they could be sure, would not interpret their duties too strictly. With a board of ten inspectors, appointed annually by lot, to whom re-election was forbidden, there was at least every chance of avoiding fraud, or culpable negligence.

We are unfortunately without any information which will help us to decide from what class of people the inspectors as a matter of fact came.
† Boeckh[1] supposes that they were generally men who in their private life had to do with ship-building and ships. He employs this conjecture to account for the fact that in some cases they seem to have appropriated material which could otherwise be of no use to them; and in one case the brother of a ταμίας τῶν νεωρίων possesses κωπεῖς, i.e. wood for oars. The conjecture is probable in itself; but apart from this one case, which may be exceptional, there

[1] p. 48.

is nothing to prove it. Of the names which have been preserved there are few of which we know anything. Among them it is interesting to notice that the name of Plato occurs; if, as is probable, this is the philosopher, it will show that men of high birth were at least sometimes appointed to this office; and probably implies that men were appointed to it not with their own consent, but as nominees of the officials of the tribe or by the council.

In these inspectors we have one instance of the *Other committees.* application of the lot to administration. There were many such boards; every department of the internal government was presided over by a similar committee. Of the work of most of these committees we have little knowledge; but what we are told points to the fact that, like the inspectors of the dockyards, their duties were primarily those of inspectors or superintendents, though to these were added in most cases judicial functions. The city police, the markets, the corn market, were each under such a board, who had to see that the laws were carried out, and whose office was the place where all information concerning the particular matter was brought, all complaints made, and, to some extent, disputes considered.

Each of these boards or committees had subject to it a number of slaves, and had the control over them as well as over the paid workmen and contractors. The boards themselves were not necessarily composed of specialists; and it was the principle of the democratic state that every citizen should, at some time, be a member of some such committee. That this should be so, was ensured by

11—2

the method of appointment, combined with the large number of men required, and the absence of re-election. It is the most striking feature of the Athenian state that each citizen had in this way his share in the individual responsibility which attends office. This was a necessary addition to the irresponsible power which they enjoyed as members of the Assembly and the Law-courts.

CHAPTER VII.

THE ADMINISTRATION OF THE DIVISIONS OF
THE STATE.

If we are to realise the working of this system as a whole, it is important also to take into account the officials connected with the administration of the tribes and demes. For even though in many cases they were not elected by lot, yet the principle of annual office was maintained here also almost without exception. And if we are to appreciate the demands which the administration of the state made on the time of a private citizen, we must pay proper regard to them. For the democratic constitution of the demes exhibits more clearly than any other part of the administration the two cardinal principles of the democracy to which the lot was subservient:— that all important questions should be decided by the direct vote of all members of the community: and that every member should, besides taking his part in this Assembly, also bear his share in the separate administrations by holding, at least for a year, one of the numerous offices.

The Athenian state was divided into consider- *Officials* † ably over 100 demes. All the citizens of full age *of the Demes.*

in a deme formed a body to which was entrusted
duties of considerable importance. As is well known,
they in the first instance decided on the claim of
any individual to be enrolled a member of the deme
and so of the city, and they to some extent had to
arrange for many λῃτουργίαι. The deme was also
possessed of public property, and had considerable
expenses, chiefly of a religious nature, connected
with the sacrifices and other common celebrations.
The business of the deme was generally transacted
in a meeting which all members had the right to
attend[1]. Each deme had however a considerable
number of offices. The most dignified of these
was that of Demarch, an annual office[2]: unfortu-
+ nately we have no information as to how he was
chosen. Beside him we find ταμίαι, who are asso-
ciated with the Demarch in several decrees[3], and
ὁρισταί, the nature of whose duties is not very clear.
One account tells us that they had to mark the
boundaries of public and private possessions; this
would make us suppose they were officers of the city,
not of the deme[4]. With regard to εὔθυνοι who are
mentioned[5], we cannot tell whether they were regular
or exceptional officers; we find in one inscription a
εὔθυνος, a λογιστής and ten συνήγοροι, and in another ten αἱρεθέντες whom we may perhaps identify

[1] For a description of this, cf. Dem. in Eubuliden.

[2] C. I. A. ii. 585, 579.

[3] C. I. A. ii. 570.

[4] C. I. A. ii. 573ᵇ. Bekker, Anecdota, 287, 17. We know from
other cases that there were officials called ὁρισταί, appointed by
the city.

[5] C. I. A. ii. 571.

with the συνήγοροι[1]: in one case at least we have
mention of πάρεδροι[2]. In one inscription we find it
determined to choose by lot certain officers apparently for financial purposes. An ἀντιγραφεύς who is
mentioned was probably a servant, not an ἄρχων[3].
Once ἐπιτιμηταί are mentioned as elected (αἱρεθέντες),
but probably for a special purpose[4]. These are all
the administrative officials of whom we have record;
but many of the decrees which are preserved record
votes of thanks to religious functionaries who have
performed their duties honourably. Among them we
find μεράρχαι, ἱεροποιοί, four in number, who had
been elected by lot, σωφρονισταί, several ἱερεῖς and
priestesses[5].

These demes with their Assembly, their property,
their elections, their officers, their priests, their
festivals, their solemn votes of thanks, their privileges (προεδρία, ἀτέλεια), and their public records,
are a sort of mimicry of the ἐκκλησία at Athens;
but, petty as in many cases their duties were, we
must not pass them by, for their democratic constitution was an essential element in the democracy
of the state. It had no doubt been introduced by
Cleisthenes, and it is easy to believe that this was
the most important part of his innovations. By it
he effectually broke the influence of the nobles. In
early times it was doubtless the priest-nobles who
held the register of the citizens, it was they who

[1] C. I. A. ii. 578.
[2] C. I. A. ii. 571.
[3] C. I. A. ii. 575.   [4] C. I. A. ii. 573.
[5] C. I. A. ii. 580, 581. οἱ λαχόντες ἱεροποιοί.

performed the public sacrifices, and did justice in the
villages. When all which was formerly done by the
εὐπατρίδαι according to old mysterious usages was
done by a meeting of the Demotes assembled at
Athens, the democracy was established in the place
of the hereditary aristocracy. The reality of the
democracy depended on whether the assembly of the
Demotes could keep affairs in its own power, or
whether officials, permanent or otherwise, should
gradually encroach upon it. Disorderly and excited
meetings such as Demosthenes describes were necessary to the continuance of the democracy. The
keeping of the registers and the management of the
λῃτουργίαι were too important for the people to let
them escape out of their own hands, even if the power
thus lost were gained by elected officials. We should
have been glad therefore to know whether it was
considered necessary to appoint the Demarch, and
other local officials by the lot; but unfortunately on
this point we have (so far as I can find) no direct
evidence. The very existence of these offices is however of considerable importance, because they would
every year put a very large number of citizens into
a position in which they would have to deal with
public money, and take a leading part in public ceremonial; they would be an important part of the
system which aimed at giving to every citizen a
share however small in the government, so that he
should not only have the power to criticise, but
himself have a part of the responsibility.

The tribes.   The officials of the tribes were fewer in number;
for the tribe had not the unity of a deme and its

administrative duties, though not less important, were different in kind. The most important were electoral; the tribe was in many cases used as an electoral division, but, as I have before pointed out, the absence of any record concerning elections is one of the most remarkable facts about Athenian history. The ἐπιμεληταὶ τῶν φυλῶν were doubtless the officials who had to manage the election of many of the officers, but of the way in which it was done we know nothing[1]. A passage in Demosthenes[2] shows us that they were responsible for bringing to the Archons the Choregi from the tribe, but it tells us nothing further.

These ἐπιμεληταί were the chief officials of the tribe; the office was annual, but we do not know either their number or how they were elected. Their chief duty was doubtless to act as returning officer at the various elections; but we find from an inscription that they were also responsible for the proper management of the property of the tribe; they are here ordered to go round and make an inspection, to see if it is cultivated according to the inscriptions, and if the boundaries are properly kept, and they are especially warned not to show favour to any individual, nor to put anything before the interest of the tribe, nor to take bribes[3]. The duties of presiding at meetings, keeping accounts, inspection of property, are precisely those to which according to all analogy we should expect to find

[1] C. I. A. ii. 554.
[2] Dem. in Midiam, 13.
[3] C. I. A. ii. 564.

officials appointed by lot.   More than this we
cannot say.

Of ταμίαι, who are mentioned, we know nothing[1].
The φυλή had as had every other corporation its
ἱερεῖς: it is an interesting coincidence that almost
the only one mentioned appears to have been an
uncle of Demosthenes[2].

† *Private*
societies.

When we pass from the administrative divisions
of the state to societies which have no direct connection with the government, we find that the administrative officers are (where we have information)
invariably elected, while the religious,—the ἱερεῖς,
ἱεροποιοί—, are generally elected by lot; and I am
told that the same is true of similar corporations in
other parts of Greece.

It seems then as if among them we meet with
the religious use of the lot, and it is reasonable to
suppose that where the priest was chosen by lot it was
that the god might himself select his own minister.
We notice moreover two other facts.   In these societies the administrative officials were certainly not
in all cases annually elected, while the ἱεροποιοί are
always spoken of as οἱ ἀεὶ λαγχάνοντες, which,
though it does not necessarily mean annual appointment, suggests that the office was never held for
long; in some cases we find mention of annual
appointment[3].

Religious
officials.

With regard to the religious officials of the
Athenian state, it does not seem possible to lay

[1] C. I. A. ii. 872.
[2] C. I. A. ii. 554ᵇ.
[3] C. I. A. ii. 611, 613, 619.

down any certain principle. Some were hereditary in certain families, some were elected and were officers of much dignity but little importance, others were chosen by lot. The reason was doubtless in each case an historical one. I think however it is not out of accordance with the recorded facts to say that, with the exception of the hereditary offices, all religious officials whose duties were continuous were chosen by lot[1], while those who were appointed only to perform a single act on one day in the year, or one day in four years were elected by the people. This fact, if true, will show how much the Athenians were in the matter guided by convenience, and how little by religious tradition. Knowing how much the power of the old aristocracy had depended upon their religious privileges, we can understand that the establishment of other functionaries, whether chosen by lot or by election, would be important as securing to the democracy freedom from aristocratic influence in its public acts of worship.

I began this essay by pointing out that the *Great number of men concerned in administration.* democracy meant the undisputed supremacy of the Assembly in all matters. This survey of the different offices in the state draws our attention to another and not less important aspect of it. The complete democracy meant not only that the people assembled together should govern the state, but that each individual should also take his part in the work of administration. There was to be no class from which alone magistrates were chosen, nor were the

---

[1] Dem. in Eubuliden, 46, the priest of Heracles is chosen by lot from among men who are nominated by popular election.

officials to form a class of themselves. Democracy meant self-government in the fullest sense of the word: each man had his share in the general deliberations, he had his turn for a seat in the council, which was the central office of the whole, and he had also to take his part in different offices. Besides these city offices, each man belonged also to the smaller corporations of the tribe, the deme and the phratria, each of which made large demands on his time: he had to attend meetings of the whole corporation, and had moreover from time to time to fill one of the numerous offices connected with it, or serve on some committee appointed by it. It is no exaggeration to say that most Athenians must have spent a large part of their life in the performance of public duties[1].

And if we look at the democracy from either aspect: whether we regard the supremacy of the Assembly, or the share which each citizen took in all public business, we shall find that election by lot was an important and essential part of the system. It broke down and weakened all bodies so as to make of every office nothing more than a committee of the Assembly; and it also supplied a simple means of overcoming the difficulty of appointment, so as to ensure in a rough way that all citizens should have a share in the work of the state.

Criticism on the system.   The common criticism made on this system is that it aimed at an equality where no equality was,

---

[1] In order rightly to appreciate the number of men occupied in public business we must remember that the Archons, Thesmothetai, and many other magistrates were helped by assessors (πάρεδροι) who during their terms of office acted with them.

for it put men of character and ability on the same level with those who had neither. Now if this is said of the high office of governing the city, it is not true, because there has never been a state where power was so exclusively made the prize of ability: ability not always of the best kind it may be. But if free competition is the best way of finding ability, Athens honestly tried to find it. The orators might be wanting in many qualities, but at least they must have had the appèarance of wisdom and character. Power belonged to that man who in perfectly free and open competition could win and keep for himself the most influence. The test might not be a perfect one. I do not know that a better has yet been devised. And though Athens may have suffered from unscrupulous politicians and unwise ones, we cannot say of her that she was governed by incompetent or insignificant men. If again it is objected that it is abilities of a humbler kind which were neglected, and that in the appointment of subordinate officials a difference should be made between men; it will be sufficient to answer that at any rate the work at Athens was well done. So far as we can see the administration of the state was more regular, more honest, more successful in every way than that of any other city in the ancient world, and (though where the work is so different, the comparison is hardly fair) than that of most states in modern times. The Athenians obliged every one to take his share in the work, they made the work of every one individually easy, and if he did not do it they killed him. The result was that the work was done. The most

potent attempts to obtain and secure able officials
do not always succeed; the Athenians were sure
that the men they appointed were not generally
below the average in ability and character, and that
they would not deteriorate in office. There are perhaps not many states of which the same could be
said.

Injustice is often done to the Athenian constitution because we try it by too high a standard.
Thucydides and Plato have left us their criticisms
on it. These criticisms are I believe completely
true: but when we recognise the truths of the
picture of the "democrat" drawn by Plato, and read
the account which he and others have given of the
gradual demoralisation of the Athenian people, we
ought to remember that everything with which
they charge Athens would *mutatis mutandis* apply
with equal force to any other society which has
ever existed. The greatest complaint brought
against the democracy was that it was short lived.
The Greeks were apt to reckon the excellence of
institutions by their permanence: in this matter we
have had more experience than they had, and are
prepared to recognise the fact that the more efficient
a constitution is the more likely it is to generate
economic changes which will soon make it antiquated and useless. That the democratic constitution lost its peculiar effectiveness by the middle
of the 4th century is no reason for refusing to
recognise its merit. We do not question that the
government of Elizabeth was wise and strong because the system was destroyed in the next genera-

tion. So long as a state has political life, every form of government must bear in itself the seeds of its own destruction.

And with regard to the other charges brought *Prevalence of fraud* against it, all I ask is that besides comparing it *at Athens* with the ideal state of Plato we should also compare *much ex-* *aggerated.* it with other states which have existed in this world. The most constant accusation brought against the Athenians is dishonesty. We constantly hear of fraud at Athens; it was a frequent charge in the law-courts, and historians, led by the speeches of the orators, have concluded that the Athenian government was exceptionally corrupt. This corruption is then laid to the charge of democratic government and especially of the lot.

But it is surely dangerous to accept as literally true the statements of the orators; we know that in many cases the accusations were false, and, even apart from this, frequent trials for peculation are not necessarily a sign of an exceptionally corrupt administration. Where corruption is worst, it will not be found that convictions are frequent. The sign of organised and habitual fraud is a general repose and outward quiet, interrupted occasionally by some great exposure and outburst of indignation. The constant activity and watchfulness which is necessary to procure convictions, is in itself a sufficient guarantee against peculations being the established thing. Fraud is easy where affairs are secret, confined to a few persons, complicated, and where each individual is allowed much freedom of action. But at Athens every obol which was received by any official was entered, and the records made public: how he had to use the money was clearly laid down: he had little freedom of action, so that it was impossible to hide the disappearance of any sum. But I imagine the most efficient guarantee against the prevalence of serious fraud was to be found just in the fact that the officials were so numerous and that they were elected by lot for a short period. Whenever a certain class of people hold office and others are positively excluded, it is easy for the officials to exact overdue sums, and appropriate the surplus. The outside public cannot defend itself: it is ignorant and intimidated. This was made impossible at Athens because there were no secrets of office. Fraud arises when any individual holds the same office for long, or is often re-elected; in such cases the perquisites of office grow, and the permanent official has a position of advantage against all unofficial men: at Athens in the democratic state this was not the case. Fraud is especially liable to occur when officials are elected, because those who are likely to gain by the fraud will use all their influence to elect men who will give them an opportunity of winning. This happens constantly in America and other democratic states of modern times, and, under slightly different forms, happened constantly in the later Roman Republic. It was rendered impossible by the lot; the more so because the lot might associate men who had no acquaintance with one another and who could not, during the short period they were in office, acquire the mutual self-confidence which is necessary to community in fraud.

The Greeks no doubt were not an honest race, but it was not the democracy which made the Athenians untrustworthy. So far as we can see the framers of the constitution had recognised the national vice, and took every pains they could to counteract it; it was one of the merits of the democratic system that it made fraud so difficult. It was a noble attempt, and it was to a great extent successful. There was a good deal of petty dishonesty at Athens, many men made a little money out of the public service. But we know of no instance in which we can say that the public welfare was seriously injured by extensive frauds or official incompetence as was constantly the case in aristocratic Rome and England. The Athenian people perhaps wasted their money—but they did it themselves; it was not lost and squandered by the officers of the state[1].

I have tried to analyse one of the most remark-able and most characteristic features of the Athenian constitution. If the view which I have taken be correct, election by lot was of the very essence of the democracy. And the investigations which lead to a recognition of this fact throw light on a peculiarity of the democracy which distinguishes it from most other political systems. Whether the democracy was good or bad, is a question which has been

Character-istic of the Athenian state.

[1] It is very doubtful whether the administration of local matters in many English towns would stand a comparison with that at Athens. It may I think be safely said that the gigantic corruption which is said to prevail in Russia, Italy and America now, and which was common in England not so long ago, would there have been quite impossible.

H.   12

sufficiently debated. It probably developed the energies and activities of the Athenians more fully than
any other system could have done: so far as it did
this we must approve of it, though for this, as for
every other system, there came a time when altered
circumstances rendered it no longer so efficient.
But what is most striking in it is the clearness of
thought with which certain principles of government
are apprehended, and the boldness of execution with
which they are put into effect. Living constitutions
are generally a compromise between various principles. Attempts to frame a constitution in accordance with some single general principle have nearly
always failed. But in describing the Athenian administration, one often feels as though one were
describing the typical state of a political thinker. It
is difficult to conceive of a state in which political
equality could be more completely attained. And yet
notwithstanding this obedience to an idea, which we
can trace in the most important branches of the
administration, there is a prudence and sobriety
in the arrangements which is wanting in most
polities. So far as human foresight could, the
builders of the constitution had guarded against the
internal dangers which might arise. The Athenian
democracy is as a work of art unsurpassed: it has
the great characteristic of all good work, in every
detail we find laborious endeavour to express a
clear and definite idea: and the result is so simple
and so harmonious that it is only after a somewhat
minute examination that we discover the labour
expended on it. The conditions which made this

possible will probably never occur again; but the scientific value of the experiment is great: it was the first democracy: the word Democracy was invented as a name for it: all other democracies in Greece were a more or less successful imitation of it, and if we want to know what a complete democracy is we can do nothing better than analyse it. If we do this we shall understand how far any modern country is from being a true democracy, and we shall also see how as states become more democratic they develope the most characteristic features of Athens. It would hardly be an exaggeration to say that a *Ancient* state begins to be democratic when the objects for *and modern de-* which election by lot was introduced first become a *mocracies.* conscious object of desire. We see this clearly in America. Elective assemblies are essentially undemocratic. In America, where the feeling is more democratic than the machinery, we are told that a recognition of this is growing, and it is becoming unusual to re-elect Congress men; it is only fair, as men say, that each of the local politicians should have a chance; it is unfair and undesirable that a few men, because they are a little cleverer or a little more fortunate than others, should have a monopoly of the most valuable political instruction. The Athenians felt this, and gave complete expression to the feeling by allowing to every citizen in turn a seat in the βουλή. The great movement which is causing the break-down of representative institutions in the most democratic countries is due to the desire felt by the mass of the people to give their verdict on each important act, and to make of the assemblies a com-

mittee in which business should be arranged so as to
be brought directly before the people. The English
are in a confused way aiming at this. In the states
of North America a closer approach is made to it by
restricting very closely the powers of the state
governments. In Switzerland this is still more
openly done by the institution of the Referendum.
If we want to see the real end at which this tendency is directed, we need only look to Athens.
There the desired end was attained by purposely
weakening the smaller assembly which would otherwise have governed the state : this was done by
means of the lot; and it is not easy to see how else
it could have been done. It is a curious confirmation of the reasons I have given why there was
no party government at Athens, that in Switzerland,
where direct government by the people is less re-
mote than in any other country, the Executive
Council is in no way a party body.

But if in some modern states the peoples are in
the way to win for themselves the full and direct
sovereignty, they are still far from imitating the
other characteristic of the Athenian Democracy.
There, as we have seen, not only did the people col-
lectively rule the state, but also these same men
individually had, each in his turn, a share in the
experience and responsibility of office. The central-
ised bureaucracy of the modern democratic state is
far distant from what the Greeks called democracy.
There if a man was a full citizen, he had not merely
from time to time to give a silent and irresponsible
vote in the Assembly or the law courts ; he had to

experience the honours and dangers of office. This could only be because the Athenian democracy was an aristocracy. It had all the characteristics of an aristocracy. It made the assumption that each citizen had the time and ability to undertake public duties. It was there held true that no man could be a good citizen whose life was fully occupied in earning the bare necessities of life. The Athenians had in fact that respect for leisure which is so characteristic of an aristocracy. Hard work was with them a disqualification. Men did not believe in the dignity of labour. The existence of the democracy depended on slavery. Slavery is now impossible. Our modern democracies are no more aristocratic. If they ever become so, it will be when the use of machinery is so far developed and society reorganised in such a way that the greater part of the population will be able, as the wealthy classes now do, to devote a portion of their ample leisure, not only to the discussion of political questions but also to the management of public business.

APPENDIX.

ON THE Πολιτεία τῶν Ἀθηναίων.

Early history of the Lot, p. 88 etc.

IT has generally been maintained that the lot was not used at Athens before Cleisthenes (so Grote, Hermann, Busolt, Gilbert, Dunker, Lugebil, Müller-Strübing). Schömann recognised that this could not be considered in any way certain; and Fustel de Coulanges, by reasoning which had never been answered, contended that it was probably an institution of very great antiquity. This view is supported by Aristotle. In ch. 4 he describes a constitution attributed to Draco: in it all officials are chosen by lot. βουλεύειν δὲ τετρακοσίους καὶ ἕνα τοὺς λαχόντας ἐκ τῆς πολιτείας· κληροῦσθαι δὲ καὶ ταύτην καὶ τὰς ἄλλας ἀρχὰς τοὺς ὑπὲρ τριάκοντα ἔτη γεγονότας. It would, however, be very unwise to build any argument on this: for, as I hope to show elsewhere, there are serious reasons for doubting the authority of the whole passage. Even, however, if this statement be not genuine it does not much affect the particular matter; for in ch. 8 we are told that Solon τὰς ἀρχὰς ἐποίησε κληρωτὰς ἐκ προκρίτων, οὓς ἑκάστη προκρίνει τῶν φυλῶν, and in Ar. *polit.* II. 12 we are told that Solon made no change in the manner of electing the magistrates. So, whether ch. 4 be genuine or not, we have considerable authority that the lot is older than Solon. Fustel de

Coulanges had argued that this must be the case, for the lot being an institution of religious origin must be of great antiquity. This is an interesting and valuable confirmation of his whole method.

As to the details of the constitution before Draco, there is of course no authentic tradition. In the times of Solon the lot does not appear to have had much political importance, and during the following period it seems almost to have fallen out of use so far as the Archonship is concerned. It appears that in the contests for the Archonship after Solon direct election must have been practised, and for the 26 years after the expulsion of the Peisistratidae the lot was not used (ch. 22). The method of statement seems, however, to imply that during the tyranny Archons were chosen by † the lot. If this be the case Cleisthenes did away with the lot, and it was reintroduced later. The opinion of Grote, and others, that Herodotus was mistaken when he says that Callimachus was chosen Polemarch by lot, is then supported : on the other hand, it was reintroduced before the Archonship of Themistocles and Aristeides. The argument therefore that the lot cannot have been introduced till later, for otherwise Themistocles would not have been archon, must be dismissed. At this time the lot was only used to decide which of a limited number of men nominated by the tribes should be appointed. Under Solon each of the 4 tribes nominated ($\pi\rho o\kappa\rho\acute{\iota}\nu\epsilon\iota\nu$) 10 ; and from these 40 the 9 Archons were chosen by lot [1]. Cleisthenes altered the number of the tribes to ten, and when the lot was reintroduced, each tribe nominated either 50 or, more probably, 10 (ch. 22 with Mr Kenyon's note).

[1] We can now understand to what Isocrates was referring in the passage quoted on p. 39.

Originally only πεντακοσιομέδιμνοι were eligible to the Archonship; at some unknown period ἱππεῖς were admitted[1]. It was not till 457 that ζευγῖται could hold this office. Apparently the law which required this qualification was never repealed, but practically it was not put into force (ch. 7).

What is of greatest importance, however, Aristotle never tells us: *i.e.* when the lot was first used for the previous nomination by the tribes instead of popular election. In ch. 8 he tells us that the change was made, but gives nowhere any information as to the date.

The account of the Areopagus in ch. 23 is valuable, *Areopa-* for it shows that although the council consisted of men *gus, p. 46.* who had been Archons, and the lot was used in the election of Archons, the Areopagus during the Persian wars still showed more energy than the στρατηγοί. It ought to be remembered however, that at this time most of those who sat in the Areopagus must have been Archons before the year 487. The fall of the Areopagus would coincide with the time when the last of this generation had died out.

From ch. 55 we learn that the 6 Thesmothetai with their γραμματεύς and the 3 other Archons were chosen as a college of 10, one from each tribe.

The statement of chapter 8, τὰς δ' ἀρχὰς ἐποίησε κληρωτὰς ἐκ προκρίτων, seems to apply not only to the Archonship. The other offices which existed at that time must also have been filled in the same way. These were, as we learn from ch. 7, the ταμίαι, the πωληταί, the

[1] This was perhaps in the time of Cleisthenes. It is possible however that the word πεντακοσίων in ch. 22 is a corruption, and the sentence gave the property qualification. I have suggested ἐκ τῶν προκριθέντων ὑπὸ τοῦ δήμου τῶν πεντακοσιομεδίμνων. *Classical Review*, March, 1891.†

ἕνδεκα, and the κωλακρέται. It was not, I believe, known before that the first three of these offices were of such antiquity. The early use of the lot for them is remarkable. It appears also that the members of the βουλή of 400 were selected by lot from the commencement, though probably with the same precautions as were provided in *p.* 47, *n.* 1. the case of the Archons. I must therefore withdraw the statement on the subject which I made in the text. Fustel de Coulanges' suggestion which I have rejected will now require careful consideration.

The main thesis contained in the text of the essay is supported by this new work. I will only call attention to the following points :

p. 21 *etc.* (1) There is nothing to support the attempt to show that the government of Athens was in the hands of an elected official, whether στρατηγός or ταμίας. It is however only fair to say that in many parts the work is extremely defective. It contains practically no account of the constitutions between the years 457 and 412 ; for the continuous narrative ceases with the former year, and the constitution described at the end of the work is the constitution of the latter half of the 4th century, which was in many ways a very different thing.

† It is very strange that no mention is made of the ταμίας τῆς κοινῆς προσόδου. For this work was apparently written at the very time when this office was of its greatest importance, during the time of Lycurgus. It is not improbable that in ch. 43 for τοῦ τῶν κρηνῶν ἐπιμελητοῦ we should read τῶν κοινῶν. It is true that the title οἱ τῶν κρηνῶν ἐπιμεληταί does occur in the *Politics* ; nor do I know of any direct authority for the expression ὁ τῶν κοινῶν ἐπιμελητής. This official would however be much more naturally coupled with the ταμίας τῶν στρατιωτικῶν and the οἱ ἐπὶ τὸν θεωρικόν

than a merely subordinate official who looked after the
water-supply. Besides, the water-supply was no part
of the διοίκησις.

(2) The account of the βουλή represents it as *Council,*
chiefly occupied with the δοκιμασία and trial of magis- *p. 57 etc.*
trates, i.e. with judicial duties and with administration,
συνδιοικεῖ δὲ καὶ ταῖς ἄλλαις ἀρχαῖς τὰ πλεῖστα. Its
probouleutic functions are not treated as of any great
importance (ch. 45). At one time it was κυρία καὶ
χρήμασιν ζημιῶσαι καὶ ἀποκτεῖναι. This power was taken
away from it.

(3) We are told that originally nearly all officials *Demes.* †
were chosen by the demes : but, owing to corruption,
later all were chosen by the tribes except the βουλευταί
and the φρουροί. For these offices the preliminary
election was always by demes. This confirms the
suggestion, which was I believe originally made by
Kirchhoff, that I have adopted in the text. *pp. 54—*
The establishment of this point is of some importance. *56.*
It would be much easier to maintain the principle of
rotation when the elections were managed by small
societies, where every individual was known. As the
final decision between the candidates was by lot, the
elections could not have any party importance. What
each deme had to do therefore was to nominate each year
at least twice the number of men that would eventually be
chosen from that deme. Now if the principle of rotation
were really maintained it would probably as a rule scarcely
be necessary to have recourse to the lot ; men would be
elected more or less in order of seniority ; the lot would
not be more important than it was when used at Rome
under the Empire to decide which of two men of equal
standing should have his province first. In many cases
the Demarch would probably nominate 6 or 8 or 10 of

the members next on the list, and there would be no competition. This will explain how it happens that

p. 56. father and son, or two brothers serve together. Twice as many must have been nominated as there were members, so as to leave plenty for the ἐπιλάχησις. Perhaps the arrangement was that each deme nominated twice the required number: half were chosen, and the other half were ready to serve if necessary.

Rotation, p. 89.   (4) In ch. 4 we have a statement of the principle of rotation clearer than anything hitherto known.

κληροῦσθαι δὲ καὶ ταύτην καὶ τὰς ἄλλας ἀρχὰς τοὺς ὑπὲρ τριάκοντα ἔτη γεγονότας, καὶ δὶς τὸν αὐτὸν μὴ ἄρχειν πρὸ τοῦ πάντ[ας περι]ελθεῖν· τότε δὲ πάλιν ἐξ ὑπαρχῆς κληροῦν.

This is not the less valuable if, as is probable, it is only by an anachronism that it is attributed to Draco. It ought finally to set at rest any doubt as to what the object of the lot was.

Ch. 24.   Aristotle dwells on the great number of public officers there were at Athens; besides the guards, and the Council of 500, there were in all at one time 1400 officials.   This again supports the view that every Athenian citizen must have held office in turn.

The passage is such a valuable illustration of the principle laid down in the text that it will be well to quote it :

συνέβαινεν γὰρ ἀπὸ τῶν φόρων καὶ τῶν τελῶν καὶ τῶν συμμάχων πλείους ἢ δισμυρίους ἄνδρας τρέφεσθαι, δικασταὶ μὲν γὰρ ἦσαν ἑξακισχίλιοι, τοξόται δ᾿ ἑξακόσιοι καὶ χίλιοι, καὶ πρὸς τούτοις ἱππεῖς χίλιοι καὶ διακόσιοι, βουλὴ δὲ πεντακόσιοι, καὶ φρουροὶ νεωρίων πεντακόσιοι, καὶ πρὸς τούτοις ἐν τῇ πόλει φρουροὶ πεντήκοντα, ἀρχαὶ δ᾿ ἔνδημοι μὲν εἰς ἑπτακοσίους ἄνδρας, ὑπερόριοι δ᾿ εἰς ἑπτακοσίους.

It is impossible at once to estimate the value of the new account given of the different offices. I will only point out:

(1) With regard to the λογισταί. These were of two kinds:

(a) 10 elected from members of the council, who λογισταί, † had to draw up the accounts of each office (κληροῦσι δὲ *pp.* 125 *etc.* καὶ λογιστὰς ἐξ αὐτῶν οἱ βουλευταὶ δέκα τοὺς λογιουμένους τ[αῖς ἀρ]χαῖς κατὰ τὴν πρυτανείαν ἑκάστην).

(b) There were besides 10 εὔθυνοι with 20 πάρεδροι, and 10 λογισταί with 10 συνήγοροι who were occupied with the εὔθυνα of the magistrates (ch. 54).

This supports the view I have taken that the λογισταί had other duties besides those immediately connected with the εὔθυνα. The actual arrangements are however different from what they were in the 5th century.

(2) The plans of the temples were originally βουλή, criticised by the βουλή: but, as their decision was not *p.* 107. impartial, the matter was afterwards handed over to a δικαστήριον.

The council exercised also a general superintendence over all public buildings (ἐξέταζεν δὲ καὶ τὰ οἰκοδήματα τὰ δημόσια πάντα, ch. 46).

The architects for the ships, as for the public buildings, were elected by the people (ch. 46), and the τριηροποιοί were elected by the council (*ib.*). *p.* 160

(3) The accounts of the πωληταί, ἀποδέκται, and ἕνδεκα, though rather fuller than what we possessed, agree with what was known before.

It is however definitely stated that the council had *p.* 139. to decide to whom the taxes should be leased (κατακυροῦσιν ὅτῳ ἂν ἡ βουλὴ χειροτονήσῃ, ch. 47). He adds a full account of the different documents to be drawn up by the πωληταί.

Doki-
masia,
pp. 96 *etc.*   (4) Ch. 55. The account given of the δοκιμασία is remarkable. It seems to point to a very great increase of the arbitrary power of the Dicasts to reject a man without reason, even if he were not accused. We are, however, especially told that this was not the former practice. This implies a greater use of the freedom of rejection on indefinite grounds than I had supposed. It supports, however, my contention that this use was a late development.

After describing the formal question and answer ἐπειδὰν δὲ παρασχῆται τοὺς μάρτυρας ἐπερωτᾷ, τούτου βούλεταί τις κατηγορεῖν; κἂν μὲν ᾖ τις κατήγορος, δοὺς κατηγορίαν καὶ ἀπολογίαν, οὕτω δίδωσιν ἐν μὲν τῇ βουλῇ τὴν ἐπιχειροτονίαν, ἐν δὲ τῷ δικαστηρίῳ, τὴν ψῆφον· ἐὰν δὲ μηδεὶς βούληται κατηγορεῖν, εὐθὺς δίδωσι τὴν ψῆφον· καὶ πρότερον μὲν εἰς ἐνέβαλλε τὴν ψῆφον, νῦν δ᾽ ἀνάγκη πάντας ἔστι δια*ψηφίζεσθαι περὶ αὐτῶν, ἵνα ἄν τις πονηρὸς ὢν ἀπαλλάξῃ τοὺς κατηγόρους, ἐπὶ τοῖς δικασταῖς γένηται τοῦτον ἀποδοκιμάσαι.

p. 133.   (5) The law that only πεντακοσιομέδιμνοι were eligible as ταμίαι, though never repealed, was, we are told, not really enforced.

οἱ ταμίαι τῆς Ἀθηνᾶς εἰσὶ μὲν δέκα κληρωτοί, εἷς ἐκ τῆς φυλῆς, ἐκ πεντακοσιομεδίμνων κατὰ τὸν Σόλωνος νόμ[ον, ἔτι γὰρ ὁ ν]όμος κύριός ἐστιν, ἄρχει δ᾽ ὁ λαχὼν κἂν πάνυ πένης ᾖ (ch. 47).

APPENDIX II.

Busolt = Busolt-Swoboda, *Griechische Staatskunde.*
Gilbert = *Handbuch der Griechischen Staatsaltertümer*, 2nd
    edition.
Glotz = Article *Sortitio* in Daremberg-Saglio.
Sundwall = *Epigraphische Beiträge.* (*Klio*: Beiheft 4.)
S.I.G. = Dittenberger, *Sylloge*, 3rd edition.
    Tod = *Greek Historical Inscriptions.*

Page 6 n. Headlam used Blass's text. The passage
is iv. 14 in Kenyon's edition.

Page 8 n. 1. Even these passages need not be taken
wholly seriously: a slight tincture of irony is surely
unmistakeable.

Page 11. It is often argued (e.g. by Heisterbergk,
p. 21, who rebukes Headlam for not taking the point)
that the very existence of δοκιμασία disproves the supposed religious significance of the lot: for such an obvious
"Kompetenzkonflikt" between the will of God and the
official scrutiny would be unthinkable. Fustel de Coulanges was evidently afraid of this kind of argument, for
he takes cover from it in a cloud of eloquent sophistries—
which are eminently worth reading (*La Cité antique*,
p. 217). But it is really a very common and a very
simple trap, dependent for its effect on the assumption
that we can know what will—or will not—shock the
sensibility of men or peoples who profess a different form
of religious error from our own. There is a palmary
example in a recent book of lectures on Greek philosophy,

where it is quite seriously maintained that the Socrates
of the *Apology* did not believe in immortality because he
made a joke about finding new victims to cross-examine
in the next world. Now any Scotsman, accustomed to
the robust—and sincere—piety which is "at home in
Zion," knows that a belief in immortality cannot be
disproved on *that* ground. On the other hand, Headlam's
argument appears to be sound: our knowledge of
Athenian orators and their audiences is of a kind which
justifies his conclusion.

Page 15. See Hermann-Swoboda I. iii. pp. 139, 140
for other cities where the lot is known to have been
used: he names Thebes, Delphi, Tenos, Delos, Heraea,
Magnesia on the Maeander, and (doubtfully) Smyrna. (See
Glotz, *Sortitio*, 1414 ff.) No doubt Athenian influence
accounts for its adoption in some of these cities. It may
be worth while to remark that its use is not confined to
Greece. It was common in the democracies of medieval
Italy. In the 13th century Ezzelino da Romano introduced it in Verona for all paid offices. After the
introduction of *imborsazione* in Florence (1323) it was
adopted by most of the free cities of Tuscany and the
Papal States, where it continued in use, according to
Sismondi, till his own time. In the Swiss democracies
it was not so common; but it is found in Glarus and in
Schwyz in the 17th century. It is also found in Venice,
in the form of sortition of electors (so also in Lucca);
and in Basel it was introduced as late as 1718—for the
same reason as in Heraea—except for the Burgomaster
and ambassadors. See Roscher, *Politik*, p. 368 ff., where
authorities are cited and other examples given.

Page 21. A curious slip: Pericles was duly re-elected
at the next ἀρχαιρεσίαι (Thuc. ii. 65).

Page 22. One of the things which particularly

delighted certain of Headlam's foreign critics was his exorcism of the *Oberstrateg*; but after forty years this War Lord still rattles his sabre. Belief in him rests less upon the particular evidence, which would impress no one who was not already convinced, than upon a general theory of Athenian government which—it is scarcely too much to say—depends in turn largely upon the assumption of the existence and political authority of the *Oberstrateg*. The whole tenor of Headlam's essay will seem to some a sufficient refutation of this general theory; and in any case it cannot be discussed except at length. But it may be worth while to examine very shortly the particular evidence to which appeal is often made. There are two main forms of the belief[1]. A. That one of the generals was elected annually ἐξ ἁπάντων to the position of commander-in-chief *vis-à-vis* his colleagues. In its simple form this belief is not unreasonable (though unproven), but it is unimportant; it becomes important (and dangerous) when it is coupled with the assumption that this hypothetical office carried with it *political* pre-eminence, whether this is regarded as due to "autocratic" powers regularly conferred upon its holder (see B), or simply to his superior position on a board of generals who possessed, *in virtue of their office*, political influence. B. That one of the generals was elected annually ἐξ ἁπάντων and was created αὐτοκράτωρ *vis-à-vis* the people. In favour of such an annual grant of "autocratic" powers there seems to be no specific evidence; and against it is the grave unlikelihood that the demos should regularly, not exceptionally, relinquish to a single magistrate any important part of its κράτος. (1) The undoubted fact that in several years two generals

---

[1] The two forms may obviously be *combined*; but discussion has often been hampered by *confusing* them.

13

came from the same tribe is commonly taken to show that one general was annually elected from the whole people (the other nine, each from his tribe, one tribe standing down) as commander-in-chief, or as αὐτοκράτωρ, or as both. But beyond the fact that the elections were made by the people *habita quodam modo tribuum ratione* (see Xen. *Mem.* iii. 4. 1; Plutarch, *Cimon* 8; and the lists in Beloch or Krause), nothing is certainly known of the procedure; and it is easy to invent—for in any case one is reduced to invention—a procedure which will save the phenomena without recourse to such hypotheses. (Cf. for example, Busolt, p. 891 n. 3—though his reasoning throughout the note is not impeccable.) (2) στρατηγὸν εἵλοντο [sc. Pericles] καὶ πάντα τὰ πράγματα ἐπέτρεψαν (Thuc. ii. 65; cf. viii. 82—of Alcibiades). Whatever the full import of this ἐπιτροπή may be, there is no indication that it was regular and annual. (3) It is clearly inadmissible to argue from the formula στρατηγοῖς Ἱπποκράτει Χολαργεῖ καὶ ξυνάρχουσιν. Only on the assumption of what it is intended to prove can it imply more than Ἑλληνοταμίαις ...ει καὶ ξυνάρχουσι, which happens immediately to precede it (Tod 64 l. 3); and we know how little *that* implies from the six different Hellenotamiae who appear in that formula within a single Prytany of 410/9 B.C. (Tod 83 § 6). Moreover, Καλλίας ὁ τῶν Ἀθηναίων στρατηγὸς καὶ οἱ ξυνάρχοντες (Thuc. ii. 62) ought to give pause. Callias had only four colleagues on that campaign (c. 61); and this was one of the years in which there were two generals (Pericles and Carcinus) from Acamantis. (4) Phrases of the form στρατηγὸς τρίτος (πέμπτος, δέκατος) αὐτός imply, of course, *some* reason for the singling out for mention of one member of the group. The reason is often the obvious one of superiority of command in the field; it is less obvious in Thuc. ii. 13, where Pericles (δέκατος αὐτός) is not in the field but in Athens,—though Attica, indeed, was then one of the theatres of war. But the personal eminence of Pericles would justify the phrase; and in any case the occasion is one when he may well have been made αὐτοκράτωρ, or been granted "ἐπιτροπὴ τῶν πραγμάτων." (5) The interpretation of Μενίππου...ἀνδρὸς φίλου καὶ ὑποστρατηγοῦντος (Plut. *Pericles* 13) is uncertain; and it is imprudent to base any argument on one of several possible interpretations. (6) If the argument from the position of Praxagora (*Ecclesiazusae*, l. 835 etc.) is to be taken seriously, it is most reasonable to suppose that her masterful personality had eclipsed her colleagues. Perhaps she was αὐτοκράτωρ, as Wilamowitz (*Lysistrata*, p. 204) suggests. The particular evidence is thus extremely frail; and it may be added that the appointment of three στρατηγοὶ αὐτοκράτορες for Sicily, and the surely reasonable conjecture that if a really critical situation had meanwhile arisen on some other front still another general would have been given "autocratic" powers, are damaging considerations on the other side.

Mr Wade-Gery has recently made a suggestion in regard to election procedure which, if I understand him rightly, saves the particular phenomena and is consonant with general probability and the temper of Athenian democracy. He holds (*C. Q.*, 1930, p. 38) that the generals were normally elected by the people one from each tribe; but that even in the fifth century they were chosen καθ' ὅ τι ἂν τῷ δήμῳ δοκῇ (cf. Ἀθ. Πολ. 44. 4), a προβούλευμα being required each year to determine the method. A general of exceptional eminence like Pericles could thus be elected ἐξ ἁπάντων[1], ten other generals

[1] Not, however, in order "not to bar preferment in his own tribe"—I conceive the Assembly to have been indifferent to this

being elected as usual each from his tribe, the candidate
with fewest votes standing down (*C. Q.*, 1931, p. 89)[1]. In
this way the rare exceptions to the "one per tribe" rule
are to be explained. This eminently reasonable hypothesis
would be set beyond cavil if Mr Wade-Gery's dexterous
restoration of *I. G.* I[2] 114, ll. 43-45 were certain; even
without that certainty, it seems to be the safest and best
suggestion yet made. But it does not, of course, follow
that a general thus specially appointed had any special
political powers.

Page 38 n. 1. See the passage from *Rhet. ad Alex.*,
p. 21, quoted below, p. 202.

Page 39. See Macan, *Trans. of the Oxford Philological
Society*, 1886-7.

Pages 53-4, 187-8. Headlam's conjecture as to the
demes was happily confirmed by the Ἀθηναίων Πολιτεία;
but his view that there was no voluntary candidature is
against the weight of the evidence[2]. Sundwall's researches
have shown that the composition of the Council and some
other sortitive boards, at least in the fourth century, was
not the result of *mere* chance. More particular evidence
for candidature is given by Harpocration, *s.v.* ἐπιλαχών
(for the Council and for other offices—ἐκληροῦντο οἱ
βουλεύειν ἢ ἄρχειν ἐφιέμενοι); Lysias, xxxi. 33 (for the
Council); Lysias vi. 4 and Isocrates xv. 150 (for other
offices). (Demosthenes xix. 99—οὐδένα γὰρ τὰ κοινὰ πράττειν
ὑμεῖς κελεύετε, οὐδ' ἀναγκάζετε κτλ.—which is sometimes

consideration—but in order not to miss a good man because his
tribe was already represented by the special general.

[1] As the tribes did not stand down in rotation, and as sortition is here unthinkable, this view, based on *Laws* 759[d] (*loc. cit.*,
p. 85 ff.), seems most probable.

[2] That office was compulsory (p. 94), as is probable—ἐξωμοσία
was the recognised procedure which safeguarded the individual,—
is no indication that voluntary candidature did not exist.

adduced in this connection, is not relevant to sortitive offices). The further evidence cited in Gilbert, I p. 241 n. 2, points in the same direction. Headlam's argument from Socrates' βουλεία is weak. Professor Taylor's explanation is surely juster and more probable: "though the sign...refused to allow him to imperil his mission by mixing in politics, this had not prevented him from serving the city in its extremity by allowing himself to be nominated for the Senate" (*Socrates* p. 98). Burnet on *Apol.* 32ᵇ 1, and C. Ritter, *Sokrates*, p. 5, take much the same view. The position taken up on pp. 187–8 seems scarcely tenable, though Keller (p. 63) adopted something very like it. The procedure certainly appears to satisfy the desire for rotation; but in fact it would make corruption in the demes (which we know to have existed) not only very easy, but humanly speaking inevitable. It is unlikely that so much would have been left to the doubtful chance of honesty among the deme officials.

Burnet has recently maintained that πρόκρισις, though perhaps abolished some time in the fifth century, was revived after the fall of the Four Hundred and persisted at least until 399 B.C.; so that Socrates' friends in Alopecae will be supposed to have seen to it that he was put upon the "short leet" for the Council in 406 B.C. The point is important,—not only for the biography of Socrates—and must be considered however briefly, especially since Headlam did not deal with πρόκρισις. Commenting on Socrates' words in the *Apology* (35ᵇ 1)— "a foreigner would fancy that the distinguished men οὓς αὐτοὶ (the Athenians) ἑαυτῶν ἔν τε ταῖς ἀρχαῖς καὶ ταῖς ἄλλαις τιμαῖς προκρίνουσιν were no better than women"—Burnet remarks: (*a*) The argument would be idle if the magistracies referred to were filled *solely* by lot, but (*b*) the

word προκρίνουσι could not be used of elected officers, such
as the generals; (c) according to 'Αθ. Πολ. 62. 1 certain
offices which had formerly been filled by lot from the
demes were "now" (presumably from some date in the
fourth century) filled by lot from the whole tribe, because
the demes ἐπώλουν—which points to the existence of
πρόκρισις, the chance of the lot not being a salable article.
Now it is impossible to differ from Burnet on any point
without a certain uneasiness; but with due respect the
following objections must be made. First, while (a) is
obviously sound, (b) assumes a knowledge of election
procedure which we simply do not possess: we have no
right to lay it down as certain that πρόκρισις was not a
preliminary to election. And in any case, there is perhaps
no need to attach its technical sense to προκρίνουσι in this
context: the meaning seems to be hardly more than
"whom the city delighteth to honour." In the second
place, sortition for the Council, unlike that for almost all
other offices, was not taken out of the hands of the demes
(as Burnet of course was aware); so that (c) is invalid
for the Council. But it is also invalid for other sortitive
offices; for it assumes that manipulation of the lot is
impossible—ὅπερ ἄτοπον: even Plato contemplated a
use of it in his Republic which is somewhat on the
hither side of honest (the κλῆροί τινες κομψοί of 460ᵃ);
Demosthenes xxxix. 12 gives a less Utopian illustration;
and the history of the lot in Italian politics scarcely
proves even the unlikelihood of fraud. (See, for example,
Armstrong, *Lorenzo de' Medici*, p. 28.) In fact there is no
case for πρόκρισις in the late fifth and the fourth centuries.
Its absence in the Erythraean constitution (Tod 29) is
good evidence for its absence in Athens about 460 B.C.;
Socrates' mockery of sortition (*Mem.* I. ii. 9) is pointless
if it existed in his time; and it was obviously dead before

about 355 B.C. when *Areopagiticus* § 22 was written. Moreover, except in revolutionary times or during the régime
of Theramenes there was no reasonable occasion for the
revival of a practice so sharply opposed to the principles
of δημοκρατία as understood in fifth- and fourth-century
Athens.

Page 54 n. 1. Nevertheless the passage is interesting
and deserves to be quoted. (Kock, fr. 166, 167.)

       A. εὐτυχεῖς, ὦ δέσποτα.

B. τί δ' ἔστι; A. βουλεύειν ὀλίγου "λαχες πάνυ,
    ἀτὰρ οὐ λαχὼν ὅμως ἔλαχες, ἢν νοῦν ἔχῃς.

B. πῶς ἢν ἔχω νοῦν; A. ὅτι πονηρῷ καὶ ξένῳ
    ἐπέλαχες ἀνδρί, οὐδέπω γὰρ ἐλευθέρῳ.

    *   *   *   *

B. ἄπερρ'· ἐγὼ δ' ὑμῖν τὸ πρᾶγμα δὴ φράσω·
    Ὑπερβόλῳ βουλῆς γάρ, ἄνδρες, ἐπέλαχον.

It is on the luck of the draw, not upon successful
machination, that he is to be congratulated. For the
next note see Sundwall p. 58 n. 2 and *R.E.* vol. v. 28.
Demosthenes' deme supplied only one βουλευτής, so that
candidates would be few and corruption easy.

Page 56 (2). Dionysius of Philaidae: Sundwall,
pp. 7, 9. Only one other instance of re-election is
mentioned by Busolt (p. 1022 n. 4), namely Demosthenes.
Socrates should probably be added; for the occasion
when he made a laughing-stock of himself as ἐπιστάτης
by not knowing how to put a question to the vote
(*Gorgias* 473ᵉ) was *not* the trial of the generals—Burnet's
note on *Apol.* 32ᵇ 6 leaves room for no reasonable doubt
on that point. The incident *may*, of course, belong to
some other day of that Prytany, although Burnet does
not mention the possibility; but it is difficult to believe
that Plato would allow himself so trivial an allusion to
a time so heroic and so critical in Socrates' life. In any

case, the incident occurred in the year before the dramatic date of the *Gorgias*; that is, it probably belongs to an earlier βουλεία, some time in the 'twenties. (See Taylor, *Plato*, pp. 104, 5 and *Socrates*, p. 99.)

Page 56 (3). Sundwall, pp. 1–18, has shown that in the fourth century there was a marked preponderance of rich or well-to-do councillors. He calculates that if the composition of the Council had been due to chance distribution, only about 6 °/₀ of its members would have been rich men. (The calculation is of course approximate, but is made with all due precaution and gives what is certainly an *over-estimate*.) But out of about 500 members, whose names happen to have been preserved in the prytany lists, 61 appear to be rich (12 °/₀), 60 to be well-to-do; and out of about 73 councillors, whose names are known to us from other sources between the years 360 and 322 B.C., 23 appear to be rich (about 30 °/₀). He estimates that about 375 out of the 500 members in any year were men of some means: the bouleutic pay was enough to encourage the reasonably well off to serve; it did not tempt a man with his living to earn and a family to maintain. (The list, complete but for one name, of the Prytanes of Aegeis in 341–0 B.C. is given in *S.I.G.* 944.)

Page 63 n. 2. These συλλογεῖς were thirty in number, three from each tribe. Their duty was to verify claims to admission to the Assembly and to distribute the tokens (σύμβολα) for μισθός. It is not clear how they were elected. See *S.I.G.* 944 n. 10; Busolt, p. 973 n. 3, and Lipsius, *Att. Recht*, p. 81.

Page 71 n. *De Myst.* 154 is a mistake: probably either § 45 or § 111 was intended; possibly § 84, which, however, is a special decree dealing with the revision of the laws in 403–2 B.C.: ἐξεῖναι δὲ καὶ ἰδιώτῃ τῷ βουλομένῳ εἰσιόντι εἰς τὴν βουλὴν συμβουλεύειν ὅ τι ἂν ἀγαθὸν ἔχῃ περὶ τῶν νόμων. It should be noted that Lysias xiii. and Andoc. *De Reditu* refer to special meetings ἐν ἀπορρήτῳ. In general, access to the Council seems to have been less easy and frequent than Headlam suggests. Private persons and officers other than the generals had to be introduced by the Prytanes: Schol. ad Ar. *Pac.* 908, τοῖς πρυτάνεσιν ἔθος ἦν προσάγειν τοὺς δεομένους προσόδου ἐν τῇ βουλῇ. ἐδωροδοκοῦντο δὲ παρὰ τῶν δεομένων. See also Tod 44 (the Brea decree). Other references in Busolt, p. 1026.

Page 76 n. 1. Cf. Lysias xxx. 22: εἰδώς τε ὅτι ἡ βουλὴ ἡ ἀεὶ βουλεύουσα, ὅταν μὲν ἔχῃ ἱκανὰ χρήματα εἰς διοίκησιν, οὐδὲν ἐξαμαρτάνει, ὅταν δὲ εἰς ἀπορίαν καταστῇ, ἀναγκάζεται εἰσαγγελίας δέχεσθαι καὶ δημεύειν τὰ τῶν πολιτῶν καὶ τῶν ῥητόρων τοῖς τὰ πονηρότατα λέγουσι πείθεσθαι.

Page 80. Heisterbergk (p. 59) finds the views of this page inconsistent with those at the bottom of page 15. A slight incongruity there may be; but no contradiction, as Headlam knew well: the lot is democratic, or what you will, according to the use you make of it. *Pace* Heisterbergk it has no "Inhalt" of its own. See above, p. 17 n.

Page 80 n. Schömann was not quite strictly accurate. The passage (p. 22 in Spengel-Hammer) runs as follows: περὶ δὲ τὰς ὀλιγαρχίας τὰς μὲν ἀρχὰς δεῖ τοὺς νόμους ἀπονέμειν ἐξ ἴσου πᾶσι τοῖς τῆς πολιτείας μετέχουσι, τούτων δὲ εἶναι τὰς μὲν πλείστας κληρωτάς, τὰς δὲ μεγίστας κρυπτῇ ψήφῳ μεθ' ὅρκων καὶ πλείστης ἀκριβείας διαψηφιστέας. It is a statement of what ought to be, not of what is. Cf. Ar. *Pol.* 1300ᵇ. Still, there can be no doubt that the lot was in fact used in oligarchies. The Four Hundred chose their Prytanes by lot (Thuc. viii. 70); and Ἀθ. Πολ. 30 mentions its use in the constitution εἰς τὸν μέλλοντα χρόνον. Heraea was probably oligarchic (p. 38 n. 1). Plutarch (*De Genio Socr.* 597ᵃ) mentions a κυαμευτὸς ἄρχων in Thebes (fourth century). Swoboda (*Klio*, x. p. 322) gives reasonable grounds for believing that the Federal Council of Boeotia was sortitive. A neighbouring passage of the *Rhetorice ad Alexandrum* (p. 21) may be quoted here for convenience: δεῖ δὲ αὐτῶν [sc. τῶν νόμων] τὴν θέσιν ἐν μὲν ταῖς δημοκρατίαις τὰς μικρὰς ἀρχὰς καὶ τὰς πολλὰς κληρωτὰς ποιεῖν· ἀστασίαστον γὰρ τοῦτο· τὰς δὲ μεγίστας χειροτονητὰς ἀπὸ τοῦ πλήθους.

Page 86 n. 2. According to *I.G.* I² 10 this decree belongs to the years 470—460 B.C. Tod (29) gives c. 455 B.C.; Wilamowitz put it as early as 470—467 B.C.

Page 87 n. The inscription referred to by Bergk is *I.G.* II² 1713 = *S.I.G.* 733. In general, see Ferguson's *Hellenistic Athens*, pp. 428 ff. and 456, and the literature there cited.

Page 96 n. Busolt persisted in this opinion (*Staatsk.* I, p. 470), but added nothing to give it any colour of probability. Heisterbergk (p. 66) observes very justly that δοκιμασία was a guarantee not against the caprice of the lot, but against irregular nomination (*Vorwahl*, πρόκρισις) or irregular candidature (*Selbstvorwahl*); and that it took place after sortition—not before, as might seem more logical—for the very practical reason that it costs less time and trouble to verify the eligibility of one man than of many. To put it in another way, it acted as a check upon the accuracy and honesty of the lists kept by the demes. There was need for such a check; for it appears that there was no regular revision of these lists. (See also Gilbert, I² p. 241 n. 2.)

Page 102. Although it is likely enough that the average Athenian seldom thought in terms of αἰδώς and δίκη, the following passage from the *Protagoras* (322ᵈ) may serve in its way to illustrate the distinction between the expert and the plain citizen in Athenian political life: οὕτω δή, ὦ Σώκρατες, καὶ διὰ ταῦτα οἵ τε ἄλλοι καὶ

Ἀθηναῖοι, ὅταν μὲν περὶ ἀρετῆς τεκτονικῆς ᾖ λόγος ἢ ἄλλης τινὸς δημιουργικῆς, ὀλίγοις οἴονται μετεῖναι συμβουλῆς, καὶ ἐάν τις ἐκτὸς ὢν τῶν ὀλίγων συμβουλεύῃ, οὐκ ἀνέχονται, ὡς σὺ φῄς· εἰκότως, ὡς ἐγώ φημι· ὅταν δὲ εἰς συμβουλὴν πολιτικῆς ἀρετῆς ἴωσιν, ἣν δεῖ διὰ δικαιοσύνης πᾶσαν ἰέναι καὶ σωφροσύνης, εἰκότως ἅπαντος ἀνδρὸς ἀνέχονται, ὡς παντὶ προσῆκον ταύτης γε μετέχειν τῆς ἀρετῆς, ἢ μὴ εἶναι πόλεις.

Page 105. Heralds for certain duties were elected: see Tod 66 and 67.

Page 107 n. 4. For the "rationes munimentorum Piraei" see *I.G.* II² 1656—1664. Wachsmuth, ii. p. 5 is not relevant: it deals with regular boards, such as the ἀγορανόμοι, not with special commissions.

Page 107 n. 5. Only the former of the two inscriptions cited has to do with the Victories; I 318 (I² 370) relates to statues of Athena and Hephaestus. (See also *S.E.G.* II 3).

Page 108. The story of the two architects in Plutarch *Praec. Reip. Ger.* 802 implies competition and election by the people.

Page 108 n. 3. These are the Parthenon building accounts, 447-6 to 433-2 B.C.; *I.G.* I² 339—353. (See Tod 52).

Page 109 n. 1. The inscription referred to is *I.G.* I² 44 = *S.I.G.* 62.

Page 113. It was not, however, a *regular* office until much later. In Ἀθ. Πολ. it is not mentioned; and the first inscriptional evidence is *I.G.* II² 463 (307-6 B.C.). See *R.E.* vol. IV A. 2107.

Page 117 n. 2. iii. 45-6 (Blass) = iv. 36-7 in Kenyon's edition; but this passage, although it refers to orators deceiving the people, is scarcely relevant. Headlam must have intended iii. 20 (Kenyon iv. 3), which mentions the law ὃς κελεύει κατὰ τῶν ῥητόρων αὐτῶν τὰς εἰσαγγελίας εἶναι περὶ τοῦ λέγειν μὴ τὰ ἄριστα τῷ δήμῳ.

Page 122. Magistrates too had to present a provisional statement of accounts every prytany (Lysias xxx. 4, 5), which was audited in the fourth century (and probably also in the fifth) by the ten λογισταί,—a sortitive committee of the Council which is to be distinguished from the board of λογισταί proper (p. 189).

Pages 125, 189. For the λογισταί see Lipsius, *Att. Recht*, pp. 101—110.

Page 130. The κωλακρέται were apparently abolished after the fall of the Four Hundred, and not reinstated. The Hellenotamiae, who were doubled in number at this time, took over at least some of their duties: contrast *S.I.G.* 83 (Tod 74), l. 52 (circ. 418 B.C.) with 108 l. 36 (410-9 B.C.) See Tod's index *s.v.*, and *S.I.G.* 93, n. 11. In note 1 on the next page *C.I.A.* iv. 11^b is a false reference: perhaps 116^q = *I.G.* I^2 137 was intended.

Page 131 ff. Professor B. D. Meritt has shown reason to believe that from the fall of the Four Hundred onwards there were two Hellenotamiae from each tribe instead of one. See his observations on the borrowings from Athena in 410-9 B.C. (*I.G.* I^2 304 = *S.I.G.* 109, Tod 83) in *Athenian Financial Documents of the Fifth Century* (1932), p. 98 ff. (cf. 'Αθ. Πολ. 30, 2). The belief that the Hellenotamiae were elected is based upon a pronouncement in Loeschcke's *De Titulis aliquot Atticis* (1887) p. 10, which passes, unquoted and uncriticized, from footnote to footnote. Having shown that in 410-9 B.C. there were two Hellenotamiae from Acamantis and two from Aeantis, Loeschcke proceeds—"Hinc vero propter indices modo tractatos [the accounts from previous years] effici non potest Athenienses tribuum rationem ... prorsus neglexisse, sed tantum Hellenotamias non sorte electos esse. Nam sortiti si essent, complures ex una eademque tribu hunc magistratum simul obtinerent fieri nunquam potuisset." Whether this argument ever deserved the almost scriptural authority which it acquired may be open to doubt; but now at least—if Meritt is right, as he seems to be—it falls to the ground; and the way is open once more to believe what on all other grounds is probable, that the Hellenotamiae, like the Treasurers of Athena, were appointed by lot.

Page 136 n. See Wade-Gery, *The Financial Decrees of Kallias* (*J.H.S.* 1931, p. 59).

Page 140 n. 2. The *Poletarum tabulae* relating to confiscated estates of the Hermocopidae are given in *S.I.G.* 96–103. See Tod 79, 80.

Page 142 n. Headlam has confused Wachsmuth's note. The euphemistic origin of τὸ οἴκημα is attested by the ancients (e.g. Plut. *Solon*, 15); that of οἱ ἕνδεκα is a mere conjecture of Wachsmuth.

Page 145 ff. For the use of the lot in selecting jurors see Lipsius, *Att. Recht*, p. 134 ff.

Page 154. There appears to be no direct evidence that these Epimeletae were appointed by lot, like the ἐπιμεληταὶ τοῦ ἐμπορίου, but there is not the least likelihood that they were not. They were appointed annually, one from each tribe. They were almost certainly not a committee of the Council; for in *I.G.* II² 1622, l. 420 Mnesicles of Collytus, who is apparently an *acting* Epimeletes, is specially distinguished from the rest as αἱρεθεὶς ἐκ τῆς βουλῆς—possibly so appointed because that year too few candidates had offered themselves for sortition, as happened not infrequently in other boards. The νεωροί of the fifth century had presumably the same duties (*I.G.* I² 74); but it is not certain that the ἐπιμελόμενοι τοῦ νεωρίου of *I.G.* I² 73 (referred to on p. 155 n. 3) are identical, and not rather a special committee of the Council. The νεωροί appear for the last

time in the Samian decree of 405–4 B.C. (Tod 96, l. 30);
and Kolbe has suggested that the office was abolished
when the Thirty destroyed the docks, and was revived
later under another name. See Sundwall, and the article
ἐπιμεληταί in *R.E.* vol. vi.

Page 155 n. 1. The reference here and in what
follows is to Boeckh's *Urkunden über das Seewesen des
Attischen Staates.*

Page 162. This suggestion of Boeckh is confirmed by
Sundwall's researches (p. 35 ff.), which show that out of
55 recorded Epimeletae 15 belong to the city trittys,
13 to the inland trittys, and no less than 27 to the
coastal trittys. Some six only appear to be men of
means; none are known to have been trierarchs, and
very few to have served in any other office. No doubt it
was undesirable, as Sundwall points out, that the
Epimeletae should be of the same class as the trierarchs
whose money they had to collect; moreover as there was
no treasury to manage, there was no need to confine the
office to men of substance. It was, he concludes, a
"middle-class" office; and from the negligence which the
records reveal, he forms an ugly impression of the sense
of public duty in that class. But the Plato of p. 163 is
of Anacaea, not Collytus: so the philosopher's withers
are unwrung.

Page 165 ff. Sundwall, p. 53 ff., confirms the view of
Haussoullier that the propertied classes had a preponder-
ant influence in the affairs of the demes; and that
meetings were ill-attended by poorer people.

Page 166. *I.G.* II² 1194, λαχὼν δήμαρχος (c. 300 B.C.).
See *R.E.* vol. iv. 2707. It cannot be taken as certain
that the office was always sortitive.

Page 170. According to Poland, *Geschichte des
Griech. Vereinswesens,* p. 416 ff. the use of the lot was in

general confined to the appointment of priests. In Athens the ἱεροποιοί were also so appointed. There seems to have been great variety of practice: in one association (*I.G.* II²1369, first or second century A.D.) all officials are κληρωτοὶ κατὰ ἔτος with the exception of the προστάτης, while the Iobacchi (*S.I.G.* 1109, second century A.D.) use the lot only in distributing "portions" (Tod, *Sidelights on Greek History*, p. 90) or "assigning parts in the sacred drama" (Poland, Hiller, *ll. cc.*). Moreover in innumerable instances neutral words such as καθιστάναι are employed, so that we cannot determine the method of appointment.

Page 184 l. 17 ff. The argument seems to have gone astray: for both Themistocles and Aristides were archons *before* 487 B.C.

Page 185 n. Headlam's emendation was adopted at the time by certain scholars, e.g. by Herwerden and van Leeuwen; but probably none would now wish to tamper with the text—unless possibly to read ἑκατὸν (ρ') for πεντακοσίων (φ'), in order to escape the astonishingly large number.

Page 186. The proposed alteration of κρηνῶν to κοινῶν was ill-advised, though Herwerden and van Leeuwen accepted it. See, for example, *S.I.G.* 281 (B.C. 333–2), which amply confirms the existence and method of election of these Epimeletae, and indicates something of the special nature and importance of their duties (Pytheas of Alopecae is awarded a crown of 1000 dr. for his assiduity). See *I.G.* I² 54 and Hiller von Gaertringen's remarks in *Sitzb. Berl.* 1919.

COMPARATIO NUMERORUM.

C. I. A.	I. G.²	S. I. G.³	Roberts-Gardner	Hicks & Hill	Tod
I 9	I 10	41	5	23	29
25	42	—	—	—	—
32	91–2	91	10	49	51
37	63–4	—	17	64	66
38	65–8	—	—	—	—
40	57	75	15	60	61
58	109	—	—	—	—
77	73	—	—	—	—
188	304	109	99	—	83
226–254	191–231*				
226	191	—	106	33	30
237	202	—	107	43	46
240	205	68	—	—	—
244	212	—	—	48	56
252	212ᵃ	—	—	—	56
253	212ᵇ	—	—	—	56
273	324	—	109	62	64
274	328	99	110	72	—
301	349	—	115	—	—
303–9	339–53	—	—	—	—
314	364–5	—	—	—	—
318	370	—	—	—	—
322	372	—	117	—	—
II 51	II 103	159	—	108	—
57ᵇ	112	181	34	119	—
167	463	—	—	—	—
554	1139	—	—	—	—

* See *S.E.G.* Vol. v (1931) and Meritt, *Ath. Financial Documents* (1932).

C. I. A.	I. G.[2]	S. I. G.[3]	Roberts-Gardner	Hicks & Hill	Tod
II 554[b]	II 1140	—	—	—	—
564	1165	911	76	—	—
570	1172	—	78	—	—
571	1174	--	—	—	—
573	1176	915	79	—	—
573[b]	1177	—	—	—	—
575	1182	—	—	—	—
578	1183	—	—	—	—
579	1198	—	—	—	—
580	1203	—	--	—	—
581	1199	—	—	—	—
585	1202	—	—	—	—
607	1257	—	—	—	—
611	1263	—	—	—	—
613	1271	—	—	—	—
619	1314	—	—	—	—
741	1496	1029	100	—	—
803	1622	—	—	—	—
809	1629	305	120	—	—
811	1631	—	—	—	—
829	1654	—	—	—	—
830	1658	—	123	—	—
831	1663	—	—	—	—
832	1661	—	—	—	—
834	1669	—	—	—	—
836	1534	—	—	—	—
864	1742	—	148	—	—
872	1749	443	—	—	—
1054	1668	969	126	—	—
1174	2197	—	205	—	—
III 81	—	—	—	—	—
87	—	—	—	—	—
IV 27[b]	I 76	83	9	—	74
35[b]	84	—	—	—	—
53[a]	94	93	21	—	—
331[e]	369	—	—	—	—

INDEX.